I0794373

CONDITIONS OF GRACE

New and Selected Poems

ALSO BY MARK SANDERS

First Hunt
Gone Fishing
The Suicide
Before We Lost Our Ways
A Dissimulation of Birds: Stories
Here in the Big Empty
Landscapes, with Horses

EDITED WORKS

The Sandhills & Other Geographies: An Anthology of Nebraska Poetry
The Sandhills II: Poets of the Great Plains
Jumping Pond: Poems and Stories from the Ozarks
(with Michael Burns)
On Common Ground: The Poetry of William Kloefkorn, Ted Kooser, Greg Kuzma, and Don Welch (with J. V. Brummels)
The Plains Poetry Series, vols. 1-8
The Main-Travelled Roads Chapbook Series, vols. 1-22
The PlainSense of Things, vols. 1-3
Three Generations of Nebraska Poets (with Stephen Meats)
A Sandhills Reader: A 30th Anniversary Retrospective

CONDITIONS OF GRACE:
New and Selected Poems

Mark Sanders

Stephen F. Austin State University Press / Nacogdoches, Texas

2011 Stephen F. Austin State University Press

Stephen F. Austin State University Press
P.O. Box 13007, SFA Station
Nacogdoches, TX 75962-3007

sfapress@sfasu.edu

Copyright © Mark Sanders, 2011
All rights reserved.

Manufactured in China by Everbest Printing Co.
through Four Colour Print Imports

LIBRARY OF CONGRESS IN PUBLICATION DATA
Sanders, Mark 1955-
Conditions of Grace: New and Selected Poems / Mark Sanders

p. cm.
ISBN: 978-1-936205-16-5 (Cloth)
1. Poetry. 2. American Poetry. 3. Nebraska Literature. 4. Great Plains Literature. 5. Texas Literature. 6. Sanders, Mark.

Except in the United States of America, this book is sold subject to the condition that it shall not, by way of trade or otherwise, be lent, resold, hired out, or otherwise circulated without the publisher's prior consent in any form of binding or cover other than that in which it is published and without a similar condition including this condition being imposed on the subsequent purchaser.

The scanning, uploading and distribution of this book via the Internet or via any other means without the permission of the publisher is illegal and punishable by law. Please purchase only authorized electronic editions, and do not participate in or encourage electronic piracy of copyrighted materials. Your support of the author's rights is appreciated.

The paper used in this book meets the requirements of ANSI/NISO Z39.48-1992 (R1997) (Permanence of Paper) *this book is for Kimberly*

Contents

III.

IV.

V.

VI.

VII.

VIII.

IX.

X.

CONDITIONS OF GRACE

It is the nature of grace always
to fill spaces that have been empty.

~ Goethe

American Flyer

East of the barn, a slope
is a glaze of ice.
I went sledding there,
at a younger age. Now,
the old American Flyer
hangs upside down
like a bat from a rafter
in the barn's loft,
pigeon poop stuccoed to it
thick as the age I've grown to.
I will not take the sled down,
nor reel in falling inclination.
Downhill enough,
the All-American boy
flown out of me,
I could never climb
back to where I stand.

I.

Plain Sense

"Required, as a necessity requires."
—Wallace Stevens, "The Plain Sense of Things"

Plain speech for a plain people:
weather-words gray as old lumber;
old sheds and old houses
sitting on the tilted legs of wind;

verbs the cranes dancing, the snow geese dangling,
something wild dashed
into wilder brush or wood, the slow steady plow
of an idea through black dirt, the blossom.

We drive the long, sleepy phrases and
turn sharp on a country thought;
the gravel punctuates, the noun-heart steers.
A sentence like a pivot: the steel spans circle;

the cold spray a nourishment, a continued green.

*

Two ways of looking at things:

Rain falling onto your face from a black sky.
Or, the head turned toward the ground,
the face blurred in the puddle where rain drops.

In the snow funnel, walking blindly through the white of it,
frost in the beard, sweet moist on cold lips.
Or, still: an iced pond, a silver slip of creek.

The mouse in the alfalfa, the hawk's black eye.
Or: the turn, the absolute fall.
The beak, the flesh, the stone talons.

The ground, too, like stone.
Or, the mud temptation.
Or, the porous dark, the quilted bed, the dormant seed.

*

A man wears a sandstone face.
Call it character.
Call it erosion.
Deep cuts, gradual smoothing, permanence.

*

Every which way the wind:
the cattle-clouds, the skiff-snakes, the gnat-dust;
the dead dressed in green robes swaying, breathing, amorous.

*

Old men passed us bottles of home-brew and we drank.
The taste bitter, the spillage dripping from the spigots of our faces.
The bitterness we recall as sweet: it was cold and wet on a parched
        day.

Old women poured us coffee from granite-ware pots.
Bavarian china chipped or cracked: chapped lips against our lips.
The hot potion we sweetened, clouded with cream or sipped
        straight and black.
The house was a mood: damask, vinegar, alum, dust.

*

The swallow is a question mark, the fence posts exclamations.
The elliptical miles, the emphatic cottonwoods.

*

Today, the tasseled breasts of corn, the bearded milo.
The wheat ambles and jigs; the alfalfa swims nude in a blue-green
pond.
How can you doubt the optimism of hail, tornado, drought?

*

A child toes the dust and sees creation.
Someone dead smiles in the cloud.

A child picks up a stone and skims the water top.
More pleasure in plunking it to the depths.

A child dismembers a grasshopper.
Later, he puts it back together to dismember it again.

*

The metaphor went around the property.
Meshed, electric, paneled, barbed.

It sectioned the place like a quilt.
It linked.

Cattle did not wander, calves bawled and sucked.
Pigs squealed and the feeders banged.
Horses ran or lulled about, nodding.

It made the garden secure.

The city folk who came out to sell us something

had to stop at the gate where a big dog stood, growling,
baring its teeth.

*

A young woman once sat in a pickup truck
high atop a country hill, the hot then cold wind
blowing through open windows, her hair streaming her face,
the black clouds on the night sky
defining blackness.

The music was what she loved: the wind-moan,
the sky-sigh heavy, the cloud heart-knock.
The truck waltzed on its tires.

And best, most best: the sharp light like nerve-something, *yes,*
and, *yes, yes,* the thunder.

*

A plain word is a simple tool.
A nut tightened on its bolt,
the pieces holding.

*

The bull snake crawling on the blacktop
is exact.

The vapor, a heat-thing that crawls and disappears,
is exact.

The meadowlark, perched on a fencepost,
singing, is exact.
And when it flies away, and yet you hear the song,

and feel the heat coil or fly about you,
this is exact, too.

*

It has to have a certain flatness,
like old folks talking on a porch swing
under the bright bulbs of stars,
the electric buzz of cicadas, a chain creaking.
Soft words like the long smoke of a good cigar.

It has to be an observable silence, each spoken stone
compelling,
a flint,
or the snarl of a black cloud-wall just before the point is made.

*

Our eyes hold the almighty sky in callused hands.
Our ears sip deep the odorous blue.

*

The swirl of leaves
is the rattle of brown bones down casket roads.
The swirl of geese and crane,
their bell-gongs,
is trinity: birth, covenant, everlasting.

*

An old farmer danced a polka with a pump handle.
All the old and young cows cried as the music poured.

He switched partners, holding hands with a hay hook,
swinging bales, the dust kicking its heels.

All day like this: everything a tune, everything a dance.
Even as he slept, there was a rhythm to it.

*

There must be a recognition of need,
and need is the plain sense of things near.

*

Out here, water is the great wheel turning.
Listen to the gurgling gears of pond, creek, river.

Out here, we stand at the center of the great wheel,
and we are the ponds, the creeks, the rivers.

So long as there is water, the necessary machine runs.

*

Were the weather any different,
it would not be ours.
Neither the land, how it lifts and falls
the way a finch dips
or the steep to which the hawk glides
or the depths to which it plunges.
The burdens, the joys, the loves, broken things:
they would not be ours if they were different.

Anything else and we should destroy the essential:
the gopher-intelligence, the ground muscle,
the harvest-soul.

What is here is ours.
What is here suffices.

II.

Photograph of Three Sisters, 1954

My three sisters stand together,
holding hands, the littlest in the middle,
her arms like rope,
swung between the older ones.
The sun bright, shining down upon
blonde-brown heads, the white-frill of sundresses.
There's smiles I don't remember
pressed upon those faces.

The littlest was the first to let go,
and, oddly, in the long aftermath of the baby's death,
the two sisters left lost connection.
A mood like a storm bank. Words like hawks
leapt from the gloved-hand of anger,
rose to perilous pitch and plummeted.
This—a way of breathing.

The older accumulated rage
as she might have bisque-headed dolls;
the younger sister silence, sadness, and,
when her tongue walked past its shyness, cruel wit.
The older bred and nurtured a cancer
that consumed her. The younger never forgot.
Loss and need lay next to their dinner plates
like forks and spoons.

I was not born when this photo was taken.
It was my sisters' story, not mine.
I wasn't there, then. I'm not there, now.

Two Snapshots of My Father

1. Fall 1954

My parents kneel in front of a brown Chevy coupe,
their baby girls astraddle laps and knees.
Sun cuts like a razor above them,
brightness so sharp the four females squint
as they look toward the camera.

There my father is, eyes wide against the glare,
smile on his face. He's looking straight
toward the future, brave man. All that's bad behind,
all that's worse just beyond eyesight.
But, Christ Amighty, I can hear him say,
It's mine, by god, it's mine.

2. July 1955

There he is. Again. Same grin, same sun, same courage.
He stands in the middle of his wheat field,
arms spread like wings, wheat tall to his armpits.
Just weeks before the harvest, a good yield.
I had just been born, the desired son at last.

But the storm came, anyway. Hail took the field
down to ground. How he looks crucified,
though his martyrdom is a pleasure house.
His frown, all those years I knew him, was thorns,
yet I did see that grin during harvest of sadness,

like Christ Almighty himself, undaunted by Hell.

Before We Lost Our Ways

The world was small as a house, then.
It was an elm-bordered,
sun-sprinkled yard of plenty.
The noise of children raced up and down the echoing staircase,
let doors smack their lips;
ran the maze of laundered sheets
that hung upon lines
and unfolded in breeze, petals in an iris bed.

The world was a bright house, lace and wood
and ordinary.
Voices never raised inside—or so it seemed.
People walked in without knocking,
and their laughter played cards
until the lights closed their eyes
and unplugged the radio static of bugs.

We knew little beyond our front door.
Sedans and coupes, sauntering by,
grew arms and waved
as we played upon the infinite lawn.
People met upon our sidewalk
and their eyes spoke,
their mouths recognized each other.
The world was a fistful of wet gravel,
a grasshopper's spit juice.
It was all that could be lifted down to us.

Safe times, all we needed
was the heat of home,
the heat of our love,
the heat of food,

and heat was an old worn blanket called hope.
All we had, while it may not have been enough,
was what we had.

It was enough.

For My Sister, 1961

In a pool of birch shade,
my sister Bobbi sits on a blue blanket.
Awakened from one of her long naps,
she yawns until her eyes are rivers.
She sips on a bottle of 7Up
the neighbor women said would perk her.
Warm air a sweater of ice on her,
she shivers as I soar upon the swing,
wind tickling my short-buzzed hair.

Neighbor kids are apples in the treetop,
gophers running across the yard
from one hole of play to another.
Wild verbs and prepositional phrases,
they are the breathless language of health and motion.

Bobbi stiffens like a stump;
the motor of her body convulses.
Once more her stomach fountains.
Once more my mother's hands fly to her face,
her mouth a cave of concern and fear.
The neighbor women move near,
death a beam such moths are drawn to.
The kids are silent leaves, wind out of them.
The swing stops, the sun dies.

Grandma's house is hot and asthmatic.
Fans hum their lullabies day and night
like the kazoo of crickets and locusts outside screened
windows.
Conversation over meals is clicking spoons and forks,

slurping of coffee, scooting chairs.
Only after dark do adult voices take turns.
Only after dark, when I lie
on a makeshift bed on the floor
behind my grandma's door,
and small wind teases and tickles the curtains,
and the moon is the unblinking eye of God,
do I hear the phone bark like a dog
and coyote voices yelping back.

The girl in the brown box
has a doll with black hair
a blue dress   a red smile
blue staring eyes
and the happy reaching plastic hands

the girl in the brown box
clutches to her chest the doll
with the black hair   the red lips
the girl's hair a box-brown
and her lips the color of milk

her eyes shut against the light
lines marking the eyelids
lines gray and white at the corners
of her sealed eyes

and a lady stands there
who smells of roses
whose skin is white roses
whose lips are red roses
whose voice is pointed as thorns
saying the girl in the brown box
is like a doll

playing there among rancid flowers
in a new blue sailor's dress

the lady talking
whose eyes are as old
as the shut-eyed girl's.

How to Know There's Actually a Heaven

And here you are, standing atop
a stack of bales, warm August wind
washing you, comfort running her fingers
through your hair, nuzzling your chin,
her face sultry. Hay smell, green and sugary,
hangs aloft like barn swallows, dipping
and ducking, sweeping up, steeping
down. *Can it get any better?*

A haze called distance looks like rain approaching,
and music is pigs clanging feeder lids,
cattle cooing beneath an umbrella
of mulberries. The sputter of a tractor
like an old coon dog snoring.
                                        And there's a man,
older than the dirt he tills, seated on a wood chair
on a screened-in porch, sucking the tip
of an unlit tobacco pipe. Smoke
would be music to which angels fly.

Boy. Raise your hands, a cool electricity
at the fingertips. Tilt back your head,
close your eyes as if prayer wraps us
in words for life. Boy, this is your testimony
though you do not know yet what it means
to testify. Boy, oh boy. Not time to go,
but you know how to get there from here.

Butchering Chickens

Grandma bit her lip and scowled
as her hands worked over a carcass.
Feathers, scalding wet, rushed
through her fingers, fell,
and the bird was bald.

My chore: catch the broilers,
panicked and squawking;
run one to a coop-corner,
trip it with my poultry-crook,
and haul it bawling like a baby to the block.

The chickens knew what was coming.
Instinct and scent of fowl blood
sank into those pea-brains.
They screamed and brayed
until the corn knife joined

its rusty blade to narrow neck,
and the head would drop. Blood spurt
its warm stream onto black dirt
where staring, startled heads blinked.
Opened beaks tried to swallow.

I was seven the first time
I held the knife and put it through.
Grandma and I worked all day
while the men baled hay or picked corn.
We found a rhythm in the pop

that found its way past bone to stump.
A cadence we obeyed.

I'd catch and chop, catch and chop,
while Grandma's hands stripped the birds
and singed off pinfeathers in alcohol blaze.

Our paring knives slit, belly to gullet;
out fell ropes and stench,
warm and slippery.
Whining dogs, mewing cats
stood outside our circle begging—

anything we didn't want,
foot or bowel, was theirs.
The older dogs slipped forward
to crush skulls in the vises of their jaws.
Ants clotted blood.

All of this took time. Blood draining
from the spigots of necks, flip
and flop of dying birds,
wings shivering. When Grandma's work
held me at halt, I'd turn a head

into a finger puppet. A country thing,
unquestioned and, it seemed,
natural. Never had it been unpleasant—
rather, a curiosity. Like one feels
when doing something spiritual.

Even here was immersion: life, death,
and the attempt to live despite death.
Done, the chicken sizzled and spattered
in skillet grease. Fresh bread
hatched from the oven, and sweet corn's yellow

deepened in boiling water. Sometimes,

playing cards, we'd wait upon the men for supper.
Sometimes, when Grandma'd rise
to pass behind my chair to turn the meat,
smell of feathers still upon her hands,

she'd lay her plucky fingers
along the strings of my tired shoulders,
rub the strained music there, rub there, rub
there. In my head, headless birds
danced and leapt in macabre ballet

until my own neck relaxed
and a curtain fell of comfort,
of home and all things steady and peaceful.

Finding the Homestead House, 1963

for Melodee

First, wading the murky creek,
muddy ooze underfoot,
green water about the knees.
Then oak canopy's light-freckled dark,
leaves crushed, hushing air.

"How much farther?" she asked.
The dark trees, the many-handed,
black-pointed directions.

Up the steep, greasy hill, grasping
at the low, gray wood, pulling.
Then sliding down the other side.
And there, hemp-shuttered,
the house.

Not long we poked about the glass-jeweled ground.
Nor stood inside the leaning door
where someone of our blood
once looked upon a summer's heat and smoked.
Nothing was there.
Just the earth's sour smell.

"Race you back," she said.

In the Likeness Of

So—two boys stood near the backyard garden,
watching a robin dip its beak to bug the grass.
Finding something to do, they picked up clods
and flung them at the bird—to scare it off,
to see how close they might come.

But the bird, hit, crumpled under heft
of humus, feathers spewed and trickled,
the boys sorry. One said: *Funeral.*
The other grabbed a shovel, dug a hole inches deep,
and laid robin and its feathers in.

They buried the bird not to ease grief
but to conceal guilt, Cain's easy model.
This the way with boys: summer long,
hot and idle, discomfort despite
crew cuts and sleeveless T's.

They buried the bird the way they buried
memories of school and Miss Eberhart,
of disciplines suffered: of hours in a closet
stinking of teacher's coat and book paste;
of the corner stool and feathered hat

slow kids wore to make stupidity stupid.
Raymond and Debbie wet their pants,
their noses pressed to circles on the blackboard;
Gary and Jim slapped for laughing; Dick
wore gloves because his handwriting

was *illegible.* What did that mean?
At recess, the children sang: *In 1492,*

Columbus sailed the ocean blue;
Miss Evil-fart was there, too,
and that's how Columbus lost his crew.

What could the boys remember of themselves
when others had been lessoned worse?
The school was two blocks away,
playground with swings and basketball hoops
vacant. The boys played instead with dirt

and death, one worried to tears.
"Let us pray," the blond boy said.
They bowed their heads. "God is great,
God is good. Let us thank him for our food."
(It was not Sunday). "Amen."

The boy who nearly cried laughed
at the prayer. He'd been to funerals
enough and knew this was wrong.
He said, "When I grow up, I'm going to be
a preacher." So—two boys grew up

and have not thought about each other
for years deeper than robins planted.
I remember their names, the crew cuts
they wore under blazing sun,
how they sat in Duvall's barber chair

as brown and blond locks floated
to the floor. I remember the robin,
its feathers, the smell of black soil
that made the garden swell,
the heft it made in the hand

as the dirt topped over the bird's song.

If such songs were colored,
you might have noticed the warble
in the tomatoes' sheen or how it trilled
along the clothesline wire.

Why should I not remember?
I heard the innocent prayer innocently
and could not, myself, help
but laugh and sorrow at leavings.
I remember the least and most of these.

Delivering the *World Herald,* 1968

"Run, run, run, run, run
Gypsy Death and you"
—The Velvet Underground

Schoenstein at his workbench holds the shotgun stock
in the pouch his apron hammocks between his legs,
polishing the barrel to indigo. Two boys, truant
from their *World Herald* routes, watch and wait.
Headlines, Vietnam dead and VC offenses,
banner the front page. Customers may check porches
for the undelivered, but boys have no interest
in the ordnance of news—war still a distant proposition
for them. Nor does Schoenstein's shining fascinate
as much as perturb the impatient. Guns are what they are,

talked dull by fathers who fought the last big war alone,
who cannot hope to be heroes great enough for sons.
Bad enough that boys carry the burden of such news,
the grainy shots of helicopters absorbing stretchers
or of protesters throwing rocks. Bad enough fathers advertise war.
Battles pretended and in Saturday matinees preferred,
the fiction of gripping handlebars as a gunner might
defend his ship, rolled papers in the carrier like dynamite sticks.
Time enough for news and old men who do not notice boys
until they're old enough to shoot.

*

I am one of two derelicts. It's my 13th birthday
I sacrifice to stand framed in the doorway with my friend.
Schoenstein builds the sheen into a holy thing
I do not understand, rubs the barrel like a genie's lamp, and,

arising out of boyhood smoke is the thing I crave.
Dad's shotgun stands stashed at home by the freezer's side,
coated in dust beneath a dustier platoon photo,
my dad among the men. Old shells stink in a desk's drawer.
I've asked him: how many of the men died?
He answered silence as sour as gunpowder.

But it's not answers or stories I want. My friend
has bragged about hunting trips with his father;
he tags along if he doesn't whine about damp cold.
He's described pheasants falling, gold as morning sun, pins tail feathers
to his wall, verifies them into the vent holes of his cap.
I've never been so lucky, even to watch. A conservationist, Dad
works all week in fields; on weekends, he's had enough of hills,
of cornfield rubble like the aftermath of Patton. Tents and Coleman stoves
cluttering Schoenstein's shop conjure excursions into woods
Nebraska does not have. My friend talks mountains,

trout streams sprung to the buzzing of dragon flies;
says he's pissed on rocks at night, stars overhead like fireworks,
spatter loud yet no one woke. Dad has said he lived
under stars and rain enough, recounts evenings bugs bit him raw,
that a bullet with his name would have been more peace.
No camping for him, let natives in jungles live like that,
and no more shooting guns. I desire the boast.
Dad's promised we will fish at Nelson's Pond
when he finishes his weekend's chores, bluegill big as pistols,
hungry for the hook's drop.

Schoenstein has numbers tattooed on his arm.
I've seen pictures of living skeletons, peering from behind fences,
awaiting liberation from death—or life,
so long as it comes outside prison. I imagine the old man
loves the tools—the guns locked in racks
and the knives in cases—that might have saved his family

when prayers did not suffice. My family does not attend
church,
though once we sang, "A Mighty Fortress is Our God,"
and feared the bullets of God's retributive will
until we found his shots were indiscriminate.

Preferring to fish than shoot, I covet Zebcos and Shakespeares,
beautiful and unlike the willow stick wrapped with string
Dad made me—what he had when he was a kid.
It worked fine, then, *he said,* it'll work for you.
He does not permit the fancy stuff of lures and leaders,
flies and spinners. A piece of lead pinched around the line,
a hook, the weight of worm itself is all I need.
So it's worms I want, big as trigger fingers.
My friend has said in Schoenstein's backroom is a wooden box
that might be a homemade coffin, filled with dirt and turds

and night crawlers, ten inches long, enough to bait four hooks.
We wait for Schoenstein's acknowledgment to spend the cash
burning my pocket, my morning's collection for the Herald.
The shotgun's blue deepens, like sky darkening, rain rolling in.
The barometer I am falls; the weather sends me to cover . . . .

*

Schoenstein does not wait on the boys. *Too busy,* he says,
for *boy no sense.* The gun needs finished before the owner comes
to pay *real money, not times and nickholtz. Get to vork*
und trow the paper, he scolds, *or, by tam, I tell your bozz.*
The shop door bell jingles a merry little song that slaps

their retreating asses. Bicycle sprockets cough
like a shotgun's choke as the boys pedal separate directions.
They punch subscription cards and make change
as July bleeds out. One boy digs up little worms in an iris bed,
drops them into a coffee can, and takes them

to the basement's cool so they won't dry out.
Clouds darken like gun barrels, and it seems
Schoenstein has rubbed a wish for rain that turns to storm.
Hail falls like birdshot, and the percussion
on the house is a torrent of machine guns.

Weather sirens scream, kids fleeing a burning village.
Run, run, they might get away. Run, run, run.

Steady, 1972

Our simple heaven was a dome
of stars that stared and winked
like pairs of bedroom eyes.
Car windows frosted over
from the heat of one breath.

We held ourselves silent
as we held each other. What
was it we wanted to say? Or knew how?
KOMA played its special tribute
to the Mamas and Papas,

and "California Dreaming"
was something foreign, winter
upon plum brush,
snow among cedars.
We made our bodies summer,

beach and heat of breast and chest
as clutch and kiss waved over us.
Sue, I thought I could stand this forever.
I know I wasn't sure it would be with you.
What was it we ever talked about?

I remember fumbling with buttons,
how you did it yourself
to "make it easier." You lay there, smiling
the charitable smile I sometimes give
at Christmastime to bell ringers.

Was I a charity, or was that the only smile
you had for such occasions?

You said nothing to let me know.
I could have said, "I love you," but didn't—
it probably wasn't true.

Then, when a car's light shone behind us,
an apple glow, we were utterly exposed.
You dressed as I drove away fast,
and I dressed later in your driveway,
our pursuers lost among a few final kisses.

Fireside Myths, 1974

The dancer at the topless club,
bathed in soapy, blue light,
stretch marks on her tummy like handprints,
grinds a tired fourth set
to BTO's "You Ain't Seen Nothin' Yet"
and Zeppelin's "Whole Lotta Love."

Red has told me: *The answer is stare.*
Stare to get them horny, hot
to trot. Buy them drinks.
She's yet to sit down with anyone,
neither booted red-neck
nor long-haired son of a liberal man.

I'm somewhere between the extremes.
I haven't seen anything yet,
yet I've seen enough of her whole love,
stared at her for all the hours I'd care to
and did not wonder how our dance
might go. She's tired—

the sag of her few 30 years weighing upon her face
as elsewhere, her eyes not meeting anyone's,
her mouth a seam. Her baby's at home,
cared for by her gray-haired,
Marlboro-puffing mother,
the house smelly of soiled diapers.

I'm too tanked to tango, anyway.
Red has said, *Watch out how you hold your glass.*
Palm goes over the top and circles it,
like caressing a tit. Women like it.

Shows you're a sensitive lover.
Never stroke the glass up and down.

They'll think you're turned. The dancer
stares at the blue lights of the Fireside Club,
a cold flame she skates away upon.
We leave, empty-handed, and I ask him why
to sacrifice the myth, to crucify him upon
his evening's failures. He swaggers.

The world is Hoover and sucks, he says.
I won't disagree. Fabric and dust danced
in the slow grind of light all night,
the music a deep hum, and other dust
rested its elbows on the tabletops
or bellied to the bar.

The Ball Game, 1975

That year I let my hair grow long,
down past the shoulders,
and wore the first of my beards,
a weedy little thing.
Then found a pair of antique frames
and put my prescription in.
Damn, I worked hard to get that ugly.

I came back home from school
to country tunes and Jack Daniel friends,
drank my ton of Old Milwaukee
and smoked my roll-your-owns.
I wore a Stetson, gray and lumpy
atop my head, and Tony Lamas
on their third resoles.
And nearly every weekend,
at a country bar where the band
played Willie or Haggard,
I'd find a gal and dance all night.
Nothing had changed.

But in a country bar at rodeo time,
sitting in a corner booth
and downing shots of Comfort,
some boys shooting snooker whistled.
Three offered me a free hair cut.
I stood to leave when one
took his swing and glanced his fist
across my chin.
I'd been hit before, it wasn't much.
Yet that's when I took off.
They caught me again outside

where I'd been to my car.
That baseball bat my uncle gave me
when I was just a kid
was in my hands.
Master Beater, I called it.
The wood was rough and splintered
after fifteen years,
but the tape was new and felt good.
I took my stance for the next pitch.
They didn't move. Then one by one
they walked, no balls, away.

The Poetry Reading, 1977

"but my heart is at the wheel,
And I can't help the way that I don't feel."
—Waylon Jennings

After the famous poet's reading, his entourage
congregates at the Ramada Inn lounge:
a male Snow White with all his many dwarves,
Bashful, Dopey, Staring, Silly, Horney, Babbling, and Gushing.
There we are, two fools from another tale.
Too many drinks, too little sobriety. We don't belong.
She tips the piano player three times
to hear one old song: "Stardust."
More times than I know I chug-a-lug
to wash the music down, to wash away the façade.
Then, we're driving seventy miles to my house,
its little town, its cornfield corner.

I fight sleep and the radio's dull chat with wind.
She toys with the radio, fingers on the dials,
tuning in to sleepy country. What's coming
is the stuff of George Jones and Tammy Wynette.
She likes me more than I can care for her.
I pull my car into the graveled drive.
We get out under a sky fired with ice.
Inside, she says she loves my place,
the unswept floors, the sour smell of dirty clothes.
My man's touch needs her woman's touch.
She asks if she can stay.

I lie on the sofa, near-sober now, awake,
hoping to fall asleep, hoping to delay the inevitable.
It doesn't work. She pulls me to bed where,

the furnace broken, I'm so cold I can't stop shivering.
She can't warm me. Nothing works.
She doesn't understand that this is right: we don't belong.
I take refuge in a blanket and commit myself
to feigned snoring. Soon enough, hers is real.
Next morning we act as if poetry made nothing happen,
the trip back to the city punctuated with glib speech.

Young Men at 24

in memory of Donald Justice

Young men at 24
demolish whole houses, turning
narrow backs to the dust
that will roil them over.

Even had doors closed softly
(and most suck shut as by
livid wind), they hurry collisions
while shadowing streets liquefy behind.

Wreckage at all corners, vistas
loom perpetual; locality blurs
like mileage markers.
Grown old, such men conceive

sons or daughters peering past
casements of vapor or running
yards that pulsate like a cricket's
monotonous chirp.

They will note music of nails
groaning, extricated from wood
pulled down, and revive faces
pooled in shards of imperfect glass.

The Trigger

1. 1962, Summer Vacation

Caps coiled inside the chrome chamber,
the trigger felt like an extra knuckle
coupled to the finger's center—
an odd double-jointedness.
Every flex sent up a pop
and gun smoke whiff that settled
on my clothes and in my nostrils,
went to bed when I did.

My friend Vince and I, terrors on 19th Street,
had played at cowboys and Indians once all morning,
all afternoon after lunch. Even wore holsters
on our hips as we ate. We crawled through cannas,
orange and red, and peered past iris blooms—
pinks and purples—like the bruises we'd wear
from dropping down, falling dead.

We shot neighbors in the back
as they sat on porch swings or watered lawns.
Someone complained, and next day
our guns were gone.
Armed with our own devices,
we made mischief still enough,
found grenades in clods and over-ripe tomatoes,
machine gun's spray in gravel,
advanced the war and blew shit up.

2. First Divorce, March 1980

The impulse to point, but not point.
The invective, as in to see, to acknowledge,
to threaten a noise, and send the slug
in that noise dead center. Or better:
to cripple by insult, to wing and wound.
Ask a shell-shocked vet: dying
less difficult than aftermath.

Sometimes there's pleasure
in watching the bird flutter and fall
than blast things
to pulp, feathers cascading.
And feel justified. Like a cowboy villain
in dusty Dodge, the streets
empty of citizens once bullets fly.
I hang my luck like a boot
on a post on a hill. Conceal my anger
as beneath a Bailey brim, my wit
quick as a draw: *They need a new witch in Oz,*
I say, *and I'm the tornado to send you there.*

3. Letter to Hugo, Triggering Town

The trigger may be the wrong book,
the wrong word, the right way turned
miraculously wrong, the water changed into wine
and all the drinkers incredulous and drunk.
The television channel turned
when she hits the room, the radio
playing that forgotten song switched.
It may be the computer shutting down
when electricity surges, the document lost,

the pre-draft notes at the bottom of the trash
among potato peels and chicken gravy.
The last, the final, the necessary cup of coffee.

Daily dispositions are barrels we point
at the other, the showdown and the itch
to see who has the faster hand.
Ambiguity a wonderful wounding,
a rubber bullet's bruise, the hollow point
truth must always be.

Passing the Bottle

for an old friend

I've got the milk can, you
the melon crate. We're parked
on the porch, passing a quart
of Jack Daniels. A pickup
drives by, lifting a blanket of dust.
A hand reaches out the window
and waves. Bees dip
into the wild flowers that own your lawn,
dip, in and out, their little oblong bodies.
Some wind throws its arm
around the trees. They lose their balance,
catch it, lose it again.
Belt after belt the bottle passes.
Each stiff sip, the hair
on my back stands erect,
a chill nibbles my neck.
The burn steals my breath
and gives me back a new one,
cleaner, happier.
                              But you wheeze,
"I slept with your ex-wife last night.
Now she wants to get married."
No news, this. I know the plot.
I advise: "Don't."
                              We drain the bottle.
You toss it against the house.
It bounces off, unbroken.
This won't do. Silence pulls us up
to drive ten staggering miles
to town for more. Our legs

soften, we catch hold of each other.
The sun sits alone, pie-faced,
green-label sky,
like he thinks he knows something.

The Old School

Jangling, the last bells
shook the napping building
awake. Blood leapt.
Oak floors sagged, blackboards stretched
as we moved out to
the hallway's pulse.
                                        The school's
heavy jaws yawned.
Old bricks exhaled
as kids, long vowels
and cat-calling consonants,
slid out on tongues of sidewalk.
Dismissal's dust. Playground's bang
and pop of seesaw boards,
squeaking chains on swings.
The flushed air we swam in.
Then, vacancy.

That summer Madeline's trip
dropped her off in coma.
Chuck and Brad left town.
Rod's dad died and made him odd
and mean. New kids, new school
three blocks down,
three anxious months ahead.
I was twelve.

Sometimes, when I am home,
I come to see the things
I sometimes miss seeing. The slide
Lee broke his arm on,

falling off. The sandbox
where Don dumped grit down
Nancy's back. Where
two concentric squares of elms
moated the block in speckled shade.
Now, it's just an empty lot,
the building's razed,
the trees gone.
                        Sometimes,
I stand here, in walls of air,
rooms of blue and dust,
staring as through a window.
The teachers hover around.
I hear them. I try to be good.

Sitting on Foth's Roof, with Beer

for Kelly

Dirt hung upon the air like a tan curtain.
The auburn sun, a yolk
on a hot, greased pan of prairie,
popped and darkness oozed.
Sputter of diesel pump.
A yowling dog. Drone of heavy trucks,
far off, on and on, on the blacktop.

"Let's go to the roof," you had said,
to fill idle time with more than talk.
We crawled out an upstairs window,
shinnied up a steep pitch of wood shingles.
Roped the cooler to the chimney
and sat there—nine beers, ten.
In the dark, maples sipped a dark draft.
The leaves chatted and waltzed.

"We're two cans of beer, Bud," you said,
meaning what we had left.
I thought of that stale something in us
drunk, stale-something.
You'd be married in a week,
and I'd be gone.
We're sour mash, friend.
                                        I slid down,
left you straddling the peak,
can held high,
toasting the night.

On Seeing the Ex-Wife

Red light. The cars
ease us to halt.
But eyes lock brakes,
skid toward each other
through the stony intersection
of eight separated years.

No acknowledgment. Fisted
lips, mute hands.
Marble-faced, we sit.

Once, there'd been collision,
hot rubber of emotion.
Hiss and swear.
                    Now,
the light releases us
to our lanes. She turns east.
I go west.
As always.

Night Fishing on Missouri's James River

A black bank of trees swam the hot syrup of air.
The gills of its willows fanned open, shut;
its tail swept aside the sky.
When the red sun hung low enough,
the woods' mouth opened, gulped it down,
and darkness dropped in.

My friends and I had forgotten the lantern. Soon, the dark
took us, too. Soon, we sank into a stream
of buzzing, croaking grass.
The night-howling birds—owl and heron,
the gurgling bowel of river.
Hours silted about. Speech
drifted.

We could not stay. The fish weren't biting.
The chill-wash of breeze froze.
Late, late, we felt about the dew-licked ground
and gathered the tackle in.
Then felt the lure of city's light drag us
foot-blind through the brush.

Last Practice

". . . men who hate to lose as much
as I do."
—Gary Gildner, "First Practice"

Coach came into the locker room
where smell of sweat and Safe Guard soap
souped the air. "Chalk talk," he barked,
and we watched as the dusty lines
of plays and formations went up.
We heard friends called "Retards" and that
"Winners never quit, and quitters never win."
And believed.
                    Next morning we hit the fields,
bruised and bled for Coach's glory,
and celebrated mud-given rites
in showers and foot powder.
Then, two weeks into the season, a kidney problem
took me out of practice. Coach knew why,
but quitters never win. I stopped getting dates
and going to after-game parties.
Gut drills and wind sprints: I
did not run. Jokes punched me
where the old balls used to be.

Years passed. I graduated into life after.
On their farms old classmates wallow in debt,
unhappy husbands and wives
who divorce and remarry.
The news is Coach quit
to become a used-car salesman.
Yearbooks and trophies pass on to attics,
but I go on to greater things. Damn it! Watch me.

III.

Traveling to the Big Empty

is first a turn inward.
The getting comfortable with awkward self-consciousness.
Or knocking heads with loss,
absence a hailstorm of words
wiping clear the fields of the unspeakable.
And seeing it all, then, as a thing beautiful.

Hideous nothing is everything of value:
the cat staring as at the unseen ghost,
knowing that it's there, as a past written
or as the inevitable turn at the next corner.
It's being haunted and the fear of sleep
and the fear of life and of missing it.

Soon enough the trip outward comes,
to the territory of all things significant, even there.
All the inflection, all the inference,
from the singing drop of rain to the deluge,
the solitary snowflake or the white out.
The night breathes like a man leaving us,

and the day yawns because the departure
was nothing, after all, unusual.
The plains are the flat line of a heart beat
and every pitch of hill or mountain the man revived.
Electricity in the world is the spark of blackbird,
the shock of wren. And we bear witness.

The Evening News

Sitting down on the front porch, he laid
the shotgun across his lap like the evening newspaper.
His mindless fingers picked at the stock, at shellac.
He smiled the way he always did—at nothing.

Perhaps the sun hidden behind the cedar shelter
like a cock pheasant made him grin,
the hour a pink-purple bruise, cicadas just turning on,
their gears grinding like an old truck's

or radio's static warming up to a tune.
Could he know the grin was a mistake,
that his wife, standing there, facing him,
had worn her own perplexed look for fifteen years?

Her face was paralysis, tongue a key locked
inside its own box. When speech moved,
like unpropped cords of firewood,
it wasn't what was said, but the amount of it.

Several days, the mailman stuffed the roadside box
with letters and papers. When it could take no more,
he drove into the yard, irked at delay.
There they were: sudden news, headlines.

December 1944

Anna Shultz emerges from her house to retrieve
the Norfolk *Daily News.* Hengstler, the mortician,
drives down the street in his new Dodge. Anna
does not return his wave. She shuts the door
like the lid to a coffin. At the kitchen table,
where a photograph of her son sits, she drinks
a cup of coffee, bites a roll like a bullet.

Gordie Raff, halfback at Creighton High,
sleeps late. "If you want something to eat
today," his mother yells, "get up to butcher
that old rooster." Gordie rolls over,
sleep sticking to him. He's hungover;
a little blood will wake him. A war's
going on. Glenn Miller just went down.

Bob Geslar in his pickup creeps into town,
milk cans and cream cans clanking.
At Sloane's Creamery he buys four dozen
eggs. "Mom's hens won't lay," he tells them.
Sloane knows the answer. "Not enough mash."
They load a hundred pounds, and oyster shell.
Then on to Fynk's Market for flour and coffee.

Bill Haskin, his folks the first settlers
in Knox County, shows up at the pool hall
with arrowheads, three of them nearly as new
as the day they were struck. The stories he tells
go back years, about his parents, the Pawnee,
fourteen mules, and a two-story sod.
Everyone listens to the stories they know by heart.

Old Bill Cannon walks down Main
with a pouter in his hands, heading to Schoenstein's
to trade birds. Two stray dogs leap up,
smelling the bird, and he scolds them
in German. Other Germans gather in the bar's
basement. Playing cards, they coo softly
in their language. No one minds that they do.

Anna Cernik's Diary: Of Daughters and Sons

Papa came in this morning
angry at the winter.
He had been with one of his calving cows
most the night,
had to drive her to the barn through snow to his knees,
and the calf's hind legs coming first,
the wet of birth freezing.
Mama in the barn held the lantern for Papa
as he worked.
I held the cow's head to calm and steady her.
But Papa could not pull the calf himself,
it was lodged so.
Then the cow fell to her knees,
rolled over to her side,
her great belly heaving and heavy with her death.
Mama, feeding little Tina who slept through it,
said Papa would not drink his coffee,
eat his breakfast,
but went out early to chore.
Then he came back in, angry at the winter.
Said over and over he wishes he'd had a son
to help him pull,
needed more muscle to do what last night
had to be done.
Over and over said he was angry at the winter.

No Accounts, 1948

You walk down Commercial and there they are,
hulking on old wooden benches,
carving off bits of painted wood with glistening jack knives.

Others lean on cars, Dodges and Packards, street-side,
stuffing tobacco into the pouches of their mouths,
some lighting pipes and the smoke a-swirl when a truck passes.

You see boys fresh with summer's heat
pitching pennies at a curb, others slaloming their bikes
around the headless poles of parking meters.

You dodge dogs as they run toward you, their tongues
falling from their faces,
some scent on the air drawing them by.

When you meet them, girls and young women step from your path,
their grocery sacks half-filled. They blush,
their faces a shade of pink dogwoods would envy.

And in the entry to the barber shop a squat man
eyeing his pocket watch sees you. He grabs you near.
He's not seen you since yesterday and has much to tell you.

The Cowley County Murders, 1959 (The Deputy's Report)

It puzzled us, sure. Five dead in the house,
shot in the chests at the dinner table,
the windows blasted out.
The hired man found in the barn
strung up from a rafter with baling wire,
his belly ripped open, his guts jerked out
and the pigs there, squealing, squealing.
And all them people with their teeth pulled.
Couldn't find a molar anywhere. And we looked.
No prints on the furniture. None on the doors.
We figured he must have worn gloves.
For two weeks Boss had us all on the lookout
for anything strange.
                                        Then a pawn broker called,
said someone brought in gold nuggets—crowns.
We was off. Got a good description
and a couple more leads from some Auxiliary ladies
planting nasturtiums on the square.
Next day we broke up a poker game
in a pool hall back room,
and this little Mex with a full house
we grabbed and found in his boot
a Durham sack with a tooth in it.
Outside he broke and tried to run,
but my buddy John up and shot him
right between the shoulder blades.
A 30-30 and a damned fine shot.
He fell like a ladder.
                                        No one claimed the corpse.
Boss gave the undertaker a coon hound pup
and each of us got one of the killer's teeth to keep.

Me, I put mine on a gold chain for luck.
See here, getting yellow-brown.
The dead folks were the Thomsens.
Lived off Dane Creek Road. Good people.
Had a smile for everyone.

The Creighton Pool Hall

The smoke here is friend. The break of the rack
quiet conversation. Along the brown-gray walls,
where wood benches sit in the haze, cue sticks
stand their silent guard. Today no one speaks,
not the old farmers with sun burned dull
on their faces, nor the smart-mouthed kids
who fool with snooker, smoky silence
held in their lungs. Whatever is cool works hard
to stay that way. The squat Coke machine sweats
in its sun-dusted corner. A pin-up selling cement
ashes with age, her wax-smooth body scarred
where someone stubbed out his cigarette.
A box fan shivers at the alley door,
an old dog noses out a space of shadow.

Bladen, Nebraska

"With us it's always a feast or a famine."
—Willa Cather, *One of Ours*

Store fronts are closed coffins, here,
their pine-boarded windows webbed with dust.
A transient wind blows and hobo-dirt,
crossing a poor man's fields,
leaves upon rails of steel sky.

Stony streets snore beneath wheels
of crawling trucks and tractors pulling discs.
Each week the cars seem fewer, and the souls
who drive these narrow roads are worms
earth-locked in a Mason jar.

It's the dying who stay. Anguished
by the barbs of death and debt, old farmers
are weathered posts. Gravity
pulls the ladies earthward—see them
bent in their gardens, the avalanche of bodies.

Life to all is a slow waltz
around short blocks,
a nodding of heads. It's the shuffle of cards
at the corner tavern, voices murmuring,
the dance of sprightly weeds upon graves.

The Oasis Bar

Leaden light and smoke choke the lounge
in gloomy blue-green hue. Happy hour
is not happy but half-hearted ritual.
Old jokes have no punch. Serious talk
is the murmur of slow-moving fans.

Sometimes, a young farmer or cowboy,
lust-lonely, marches across the dance floor
to meet defeat: the women here are ugly
with toughness. When pairings take,
romance is a sin of omission.

Most folks here are extensions of their chairs,
stiff, still, new moons stuck in phase,
stationary above their planet tables.
The hours shamble away like dollar bills.
Talk is the desultory chink of glass.

When the sad hour comes, when the sad songs
cease their play and everyone leaves,
the night is foul, empty as a bottle.
The moon's face is a blotter,
stained with beer, sopped with smoke.

February Wash

Grackles, black pins
clipped to power lines,
hang on cold like sheets
filled with sails of wind.

Snow bleaches a grove
of blue spruce,
ice starching boughs.
White stings, flat as an iron.

The Significant Otter

floats on his back in icy water,
holds a silver-finned minnow
in praying paws and gnaws off its head.

Sometimes you'll find him, skiing
pond-side slopes or nosing through
last summer's fallen brush.

Most often it's just the black periscope
of whiskered head or tail,
a ring of circles on water's top.
Or trough in snow where he's plowed.

The Rock Hound

in memory of Bill Haskin

This inadequacy in the eye to see deep enough,
to sort at a standing glance the prize from the sand—.
I spend days grazing grasslands, now and then
kicking dirt in anger, now and then
sifting excitedly through a blowout's centuries.
Sometimes it's months before I find a keeper,
an agate or an arrowhead, sometimes so long
I fool myself into thinking I've found a fossil
or a geode's bony back, rawing the fingers
in glassy gravel only to unearth a rusty gear,
a root, a can. Sometimes a nephew goes with me,
half-trying, half-bored with effort,
and he discovers the best ones: rattlesnake agates,
obsidian, moonstone, flint. Sometimes, even,
beautiful little points hundreds of years old.
I've done this forever and have yet to enjoy such luck.
In shelves in my home I have maybe only sixty stones
polished down, two good blue hunks of petrified wood,
maybe four dozen white to gray broken points.
A few of these I found by accident,
herding leaves with a rake or skipping stones
on Wyoming's Powder River. But most took months
of stalling work. I have, besides, two other trophies:
the blue-green scars on my left shin—
a two-pointed one where a rattlesnake struck
while I was scaling rocks at Sonora,
the other a cross-shaped cut where I opened the wound
and bent to suck it clean. Falling back sick,
I passed out. Then woke next morning to find my hand
clutching the piece of turquoise I set into this ring.

Elms

Ghosts of elm trees picket the streets
of the Midwest, rock in age-old wind.
Their lead-heavy boughs creak.

The spring-sapped leaves that haunted
the shingled roofs of old frame-houses
spook the emerald lawns with shade.

We hear them groan at night in ghastly air.
What souls are theirs, hosts of blight and worms?
Their fatality corrodes our casual slumber.

We know they are gone, as if extinct.
But the mind's eyes see them, years ago:
like temples in a desert, distinct
as statues of gods along a river's shores.

The World

> *"—As though one had pulled a string*
> *In an unfamiliar house,*
> *Of a dim light, darkening."*
> —Weldon Kees, "The Darkness"

The World is a dance hall and saloon,
a dark place you come to, alone.
Sometimes you meet someone, share a waltz,
a few drinks. Sometimes you can talk
hours into minutes, minutes into hours.
Sometimes you spend the night elbowed to the bar,
staring into the mirror or at the bottles,
silent and brilliant, set there like idols.
Sometimes you simply wait out the rain,
and the noise of the thunder gone crazed
outside The World is lost in the drum
of the jukebox. Sometimes you fight someone;
sometimes it matters. Sometimes, when you're lucky,
you leave The World with someone clutching
you. And sometimes you just get drunk.

IV.

The Suicide

"This is not death, it is something safer."
—Sylvia Plath

The season of transition,
hot days, cold nights that October week Jerra and I make our move,
that time we put order to our lives.
We divest the corners of their darkness,
make a bright place with plants and lamps.
When our room-to-room ritual has rid the house
        of its demon-emptiness,
we celebrate, we meet our neighbors,
Mary, LaDonna, Buddy Cloud,
and call them friends.

1. Mary

For a week we get calls from her, find her notes
stuffed under our door about her business trip—
going to Texas to school for American Life,
some confusion expected across the road.
The car will be there, she'll be gone.
Instructions: *feed the dog and cat,*
Buddy Cloud from down the street will help.

But the dog turns up missing. We start hunting,
opening up the house and finding,
taped to the walls,
cryptic notes: *Do not weep at my grave, I am not there.*
                 Contact Greenlawn for arrangements.
Tags attached to her belongings read:
the microwave to LaDonna Williams,

the lamp to Aunt Lil,
the plants to us *if* we *want them.*
Legal papers and car keys,
last wishes laid out on the buffet's top.
A psalm: *Yea, though I walk through the valley*
of the shadow of death.
A menorah completing the shrine.
And on a shelf, a library book,
the word *suicide* like a small fuse on the spine.

"Something's not right here," Buddy says.
I smile,
the only thing I know to do.

2.

From the front door,
someone calls as into the mouth of a cave:
"Anybody home?" And the door in her hands
squeaks on its hinges.
I echo back, "Yes."

The woman with her old man friend
does not know us.
Confusion on her face is a sack of dry leaves
with the bottom fallen out.

I explain, and introductions follow in snips:
Mary's Aunt Lil; the man, John.

She looks the house over once,
sees wounds in each room.
"Look in the fields, boys," she says,
"that's what we came to do."

3.

The phone rings and Buddy answers it.
"Who's this?" he says.
"Ain't she on a business trip for you?" he says.
Then Buddy puts the phone down like a glass.
Words do not come, they are nails,
up to their heads in wood.
He remembers seeing three 20-gauge shells
on the buffet when he was over last.
Now they are gone.

My wife remembers them, too,
yellow casings,
the other day coming over to feed the animals,
Mary still at home,
scaring her.
She said she had a headache.
Tomorrow, she'd go.

4.

We begin the hunt where cold begins,
falling into it.

Wet in the earth finds the cold
in our roots,

draws itself up to the roots
of our hair.

Might man be a tree for even a short time,
stripped by a December wind?

Might man fail in his heaviness,
like every limb

or snapped twig, leaf which kissed the dirt
and browned?

Might be, but today my hands are pink.
I feel a flush like life in my face.

5. John

"Watch your step so we can see her tracks," he says,
and buzzards out his arms to keep us from going first.
So we stand back.
John says,
"Here are some here," and,
"Here is a dog's tracks."
But Mary's?
But Annie's, her dog?

We cross the creek where the tracks go in,
and after fifteen feet
mud meets grass, and we lose them.
We fan through the woods,
peer in and out of small places,
closed in by cocoons of limb and vine.
Recent winter rain has shocked the ground,
water stands in lower spaces,
cold easing its way into my boots,
creeping under my socks.

Old Sherlock, John,
the first to give the search up for the warm house,
says, "She ain't out here,"

and leaves.

I go another way, deeper into higher wood,
dry limbs overhead knitting black net
on a white-field of sky.

6.

What will she say when she finds out
we looked for her in the woods and open field?
What will she think when she knows we suspect her intentions?
Does dark meet us on our terms?
Does dark listen at the door for a knock, a ringing doorbell?
Does it sit near a table where a phone, as poised as a cat,
lifts the arch of its back to stretch, and the mouthpiece yawns?
What will she say when she returns from her trip,
finds we have disturbed her order?
"It looked awful funny," Buddy Cloud would say to her.
"We weren't sure," Lil would say.
My wife would try: "We did what we thought was right,
all things considered."

Would she rise from her outrage, as from a grave?
Would she wipe the dirt from herself,
ask us to leave?
Lord, don't let her be dead,
don't let me find her here,
alone in the woods, a white rag tied to a sapling,
soft ground wet underfoot.

7.

Crows fall from the woods
to a place on the ground
where a bundle of white is.
Mary? No. A low spot.
Water. Ice.
I slip over piles of old timber.
Has it been an hour?
Two? Less than an hour?
I whistle. Call: Annie!
at a barking dog I do not see.

I swim through whips of cane, hawthorn.
I breathe deep, whistle long,
breathe shallow,
spit. Stop.

8.

My wife meets me at the door.
"Anything," I ask.
Notes, she explains.
More explanations.
Directions about who to contact.
Family, friends.
Cremation.
No obituary wanted in the paper.
Apologies to her landlord,
rent six months past due,
twelve hundred dollars.

Many are here now,
looking through remnants

for a clue to where she's gone.
Many have helped her,
fed and cared for her pets
when she was out of town.
How often did she call us on the phone
to talk morning out of night?
How often leave little notes under the door?

"Maybe she didn't feel the way we did?"
Jerra says.
She's right. She's wrong.

9. The Directions

In a drawer at the base of Aunt Lil's lamp:
Go east to the bridge over the creek.
Cross it. Turn left.
That's where she walked her dog at night.
"The dog?" I ask.
The neighbors have had her since last night
when Mary dropped her off.

10.

Not under the bridge,
four rust-red beams spanning the water.
Not in the two sheds near the creek,
though, when I looked in one,
something stared back in my face.
It was dark.

11. Buddy

"Take the north windbreak,
I'll cover the south.
It'll take us about half the time.—
Cowboy boots," he says, "are the coldest things
a man can wear."

I start here, he starts there.
"What's that red rug on the tree,
a marker?"
"Nothing, Buddy. Kids playing. Wind."
Ten steps. Twelve.
And there she is.
I'm heading right for her,
or the lee she's built
to hide her from the path.
"You sure?" he asks.
The red checkered pants.
The red bathrobe.
The red hair, the freckles on the arm.
I say, "Let's get back."

12. The Police

The police descend like flies,
take our statements,
take their photographs.
Then, in sweeping consummation,
the ambulance makes its collection.

13.

Final conversations, Buddy saying:
"Things like this don't bother me much.
I owned a meat packing plant for twenty-five years,
piled up pigs and steers all day long.
Sure could use a drink, though."
(The white December sky faceless as a moon.
The pale sun oozing like a yolk.)

I say: "Buddy, it was nice getting to know you better,
though the circumstances . . . ."
He says: "Come over. Anytime."
(And walking up the lawn to our door,
Buddy down the street to his,
I know I won't).

14.

Evening.
I make myself a pan of swirly macaroni and cheese.
Swallowing, the image comes up.
The growing dark is checkered with clouds.
Small stars are freckles on the arms of the sky.
A bad taste in my mouth is red hair.

15.

When we go to bed that night
we take death with us,
wrestle it until we have it buried in cold sleep,
until we have piled rocks,
our dreams, over it.

Then we wake.
We go about our business,
window-shop,
consider names for a child
we are not yet having.
With three days passed,
we laugh about it,
hint about the grisly details
as if we were playing Password.

In January a new family moves in.
"Life goes on," we say,
and I know it's cliché.
But it does. It does.

V.

American History

Chapter November, 1983: baby wakes.
I rise to warm her bottle, the stove's flame
like the morning's blue light. Cardinals
feeding; a fringe of snow on the fence rails;
my wife asleep. Hourly darkness in all the gray rooms.

Toast is lunch. Minutes of a Henry Fonda film.
We're all out the door, drop baby at Grandma's,
and Mom and Dad go grocery shopping. In Produce
I hear a siren cry like a child;
an ambulance speeds west. In Magazines,

Life remembers twenty years before—Camelot,
Jack's somber face on the slick cover.
I was eight. Miss Swain knocked,
short bearer of short news. Miss Moore rushed out.
School closed, some of the boys glad

for the vacation and Oswald a hero. Ernie and Don
marched the playground, chanting, "Kennedy's
a nigger lover, Kennedy's a nigger lover."
That noise now like a nail in the head.
America's innocence drowned, and today's chance

sending me to Meat. I pick out a ham, some steak.
My wife gets the dog a bone. Knick-knack,
patty-whack to the checkout. We wonder
if we have enough children in the one,
how quickly she has grown in six weeks.

We have bought her many books: she
will read early. We have bought records: she

will love to sing. We take her to church: she
might have hope beyond hope. I write my check.
We pick up baby and go home again, home again

where night works systematically away and closes its notepad.
When baby's asleep, my wife and I
dance the hokey-pokey. There's a bird in the nest
on the twig on the branch on the tree,
our home the prettiest hole you ever did see.

Hands

for Travis

1.

In kindergarten, my hands embarrassed me.
They were too large, awkward with scissors and pencils,
spastic as I talked. The little fingers,
pitiably crooked, were bent like fish hooks.
Other kids called them monkey hands, and,
shamed, I refused to play at P.E. for fear of notice.
The teachers insisted I race or exercise,
but I would not join. Eventually,
I was left alone. Eventually,
taunting stopped. When the rest ran or hit balls,
my hands took me to the jungle gym
where I climbed and swung better than any of them.

2.

In later years, my hands and I became great friends.
In junior high, they lost their virginity first,
discovering tit and nipple. By high school,
my hands were experts with bra clasps;
under dresses, under panties, they taught me more
about sex than I ever learned from my father's talks.
My hands got me drunk.
They got me into and out of trouble.
My hands pointed me directions I followed
and did not fail me.

3.

Recently my hands have been anxious.
I find my fingers tapping restlessly on desk tops.
I find them pressing hard against my temples,
trying to relieve my headaches.
They're always reaching for a cup of coffee
or aspirins. At night, when I go to sleep,
they go to sleep, and the numbness wakes my anger.
In winter, my hands cannot stay warm
but deafen with chill. What can I think?
That my hands are depressed? That they are lonely?
Now and then they touch my face to rub it.
Now and then they sneak in a scratch or two.
I keep them clean, but I don't love them as I did.
Now and then, and only out of kindness to myself,
I allow them a few tactile pleasures:
before sleep, as I make love to my wife;
at play with my children, with blocks or dolls.
It's not the same. When my hands ache most, I ignore them.

4.

Now you. Born with one hand cheated,
the fingers stubbed, more paw than hand.
At first I grieved, sick with unreasoned self-blame.
Then angry, I cursed the sky down.
Slowly, I accepted. Now, when we play and you are curious,
I tell you the incomprehensible to make it easier:
"God gave you special fingers, Buddy."
Aware of my own failure, I try to teach you something
deeper than love, that perfection is imperfect.
You, with your hands working all manners of intricacies,
books to buttons, confirm it.
The imperfect world is as it should be, whole,
lacking nothing.

The Move to Tarkio, Missouri, 1985

My wife sat on the back porch step,
looking south past green hills
all clothed-over in corn and wheat,
the Fall harvest still some distance off.

She had not wanted to move—not so far
from family and the Ozarks she loved.
They were inside her, like our unborn son
she carried. I had been busy, constantly,

unpacking boxes, putting the house right,
placing furniture in places I imagined
would please her. She said nothing,
had said next to nothing for days.

In her next to nothing, said more nothing.
The silence meant a silence I could not fill,
that I could not know how to fill.
She sat on the porch step, head down,

eyes buried into the caverns of her hands,
and, yet, I could see streams breaking
from those rocks. I approached the abyss,
poised on its edge, certain to find a way

to descend safely, no matter how precarious.
Yet I fell into the darkness, fell,
and fell. No amount of me could touch
the depth nor the walls. No amount of reaching

or grasping could give me handhold.
No amount of dim-me could suffice.

Falling is horror. As I fell, I thought, God,
how I love her, how willing to risk falling.

She did not want to move. Did not move.

Windows

Two roads impassable in rain.
The third, the graveled route, the way
to town, meeting with county highway.
Along that stretch an old farmstead
sits where buildings, gutted, house
new machines, brilliant, red
in the morning's sleepy gleam. The house,
abandoned, is dire poverty.
I
see myself at life's end
like the house's shell, vacant, windowless.
Glass makes all the difference,
collects dust, curtains despair.
Had it this, as I do—.

Back home on the floor, playing
with my children, I wonder
what will happen to this house
if we should move. Two roads dirt,
the third kept graveled by our landlord
in our service, it's likely
the house would remain untenanted.
His business is land, not house.
If roads are wet, he has no reason
to come. If we leave, he says,
he may not rent. Rent, he says,
does not pay for gravel.
I
think a man's soul is a house,
his eyes its windows, his mind's-eye
the image attic: a hunter in a pickup
comes by—this is what it sees—

not a single pheasant all day.
The beer's gone, he's got two cigarettes.
Cold, his feet numb. He
sees this place, set behind
the dark of spruce, the lawn overgrown,
the lights black. The driveway
lost to native grass. He stops.
Crawls out. Looks the place over.
A pretty house. Shame it's empty.
Not one window out.
He grabs his gun, shooting one-
two-three-four-five-
reload-six-seven-eight-
nine-ten-reload windows
until the shells are gone.
Until the house, incredulous,
goes incredibly black.
A hum of pickup, a dusting of road,
a happy numbness in the hunter's shoulder.

The house sits there, like a man,
walls weakening, sullen beyond grief.

These Children

"Who is this that visits us from beneath the earth?"
—Robert Bly, "Meeting the Man Who Warns Me"

These children, who sometimes wake
and slip to my bed during thunder
and lightning's slash,
who meet incomprehensible terror
in their dreams and run,
take comfort in my snoring,
that erasure of my day-rooted rage.
They find a kind, dark peace in my covers.

But what can they know? Not death, debt,
and the heart's bankruptcy.
Not that old man who stands in the mirror, mocking me.
Day by day he is there,
stepping from shadows
to unveil darkened eyes, grayish skin.
When he turns to enter his cave,
looking back over his shoulder,
I turn to my own. Yet,
is his cave any darker?

Have these children seen that smirking man, too?
Or how the earth's full hands
tremble with panic?
Sometimes my children clutch stones of fear
and tremorous night brings them down
the crooked, leaning hall to my sleep.
Silent and approachable,
I must share this, my common bed,
the stones from my sleeping hands dropped.

Vigil at a Missile Silo

Because I did not marry a bomb,
nor impregnate a bomb,
nor watch a bomb swell in the belly
of a bomb,
because I did not study the bomb
in Lamaze classes,
nor watch a bomb crown and deliver and cry,
nor hold the bomb purple and cold and scared
in the bomb's white light,
nor walk the floor late at night
with the bomb sucking its bottle.

Because I do not have bombs for friends,
nor relatives, nor pets,
nor students, nor habits,
because I do not smoke the bomb
or eat it or drink it,
because I do not want to sleep with a bomb
or hear a bomb snore,
because I do not want to dream bombs
and wake sitting up, my heart a bomb.

Because I do not want bombs for neighbors,
nor have them park their bombs
in my driveway,
nor have them leave their bombs unmowed,
nor allow their bombs to bark all night.
Because I do not want to pick up
their filth,
nor bathe with the bomb
looking in the window,
or calling me on the phone,

or reading the newspaper over my shoulder,
or selling me chances in a raffle.

Because
the world should not be a bomb,
a nation should not be a bomb,
a man should not be a bomb,
or have ideas that are bombs.

A bomb should not be a bomb.

Assets, 1987

That round table I bought used three years ago,
its top glad with children's scribbles.
Four wicker chairs, two whose seats fall off.
A sofa, milk-stained and urine-tattooed.
Two rockers, the black one torn,
rip like an appendectomy scar;
the gold old one's bones grind and pop.
The television, that playful dwarf
my children spend hours with. Four beds:
the crib no longer used,
two full-sized ones used only partially,
and the king-sized bed that's sleep to all.
We have a washer that doesn't wash,
a dryer that doesn't dry. A hot stove,
and a yawning refrigerator.
Not enough else to bother claiming,
except this beat-up typewriter
beating up a skinny kid I call a poem.
What value do you place on a poverty like that?

Villanelle for Nathan

The youngest does not love me: he says so.
He greets me with a punch or kick. Or quiet.
He sneers and retreats to dark word caves.

Puzzled at his lack of joy, his companion misery,
I think: "Choose happiness; a stray dog fed follows."
He sneers and retreats to dark word caves.

My son is my mirror; we are twins in opposite.
My father had swapped affection for ridicule's slap;
his youngest, he did not love me: he said so.

When I showed slow interest in saws and nails,
my father threw his verbal tools at me;
he sneered and retreated to dark word caves.

Joinery should be made with dowels of love.
Am I wrong to right the wrong of a generation?
My youngest does not love me: he says so.

Bound between two silences, I desire love.
Yet, the watch-hand watched revolved:
my youngest does not love me: he says so.
He sneers and retreats to dark word caves.

O Beautiful, 1990

for Stephanie

There was wind, a scissortail balanced on an electric line,
red dust rolling in like chimney smoke from the north, across
    Route 66
from a peanut field where combines, like fat dinosaurs, ate
everything flat. There was horizon that spooled out all directions
and did not stop unspooling but was absorbed in a tan haze,
the dust, our landlord said, that would find its way inside
    our house,
fine as flour sifted, under doors, seepage beneath indecipherable
    junctures
of windows and sills. There was wind, indeed, whistling monotone,
humming insistencies that, fathomless, I could not fathom.
There had been a long drought. Gravel on the driveway
rasped and coughed. The landlord pointed us toward the storm
    cellar,
a concrete hole in the ground next to a basketball court
where the net's fibers frayed like old shoe strings; there was
darkness inside the hole, and there was a fear below me
as dark as a tornado might be if one should roll this way.
But this was unnecessary anxiety: that storm would never come.
There would be drought continued, and then hard rain
that churned red mud. Then an immediate winter, ice
breaking elms and cedar, whole windbreaks stomped down,
snow that held and held us captive before it turned us loose,
hungry for spring's green lifting little from the muck.
All that would come. Due time. Today, though, there was
    my daughter, almost seven,
standing on the porch, air wrapped warm around her,
her arms elevated, conducting a music she heard
played by the wind, the scissortail, the humming electric line,

the cadence of tires, the heartbeat of all there was there.

She was singing:

> *O beautiful for spacious skies,*
> *For amber waves of grain;*
> *For purple mountain majesties*
> *Above the fruited plain!*

Perfect at that moment, symphony soft around every sharp corner we had yet to turn.

Prayer After Sex

In the bedroom across the hall,
my daughter's radio plays, its cat's eye yellow
in her dark room like one of us watching,
making sure she's safely asleep.
The weatherman has come on to sing
his storm song: hail falls
like vengeful stones upon a sinful plain-folk;
wind topples trees, uproots houses;
torrents in the raging, city streets;
lamps blinking and staggering.

The radio man blabs on. My daughter
sleeps through it, the fan on her dresser
waltzing back and forth, humming, whispering
as I had when she was a baby,
walking the floor with her until she slept.
Meanwhile, across the hall from her,
her mother and father once again fall in love
and celebrate that love, head to head,
center to center, soul to toe, toe to soul.
The dark blueness of the room cascades over us,
the silence of our dance falls upon ears
that understand the unspoken.
Rain plays cymbals upon the roof,
spatters at the window like something sizzling.

Dear Thunder, feed us with music such as this.
Delight our bodies again and again with nerve-lightning,
and provide us with the calming bed
where love is built brick to brick, stone to stone,
heartbeat to heartbeat.
Let the storms, the ruinous, ravening storms,
wreak havoc, far, far, far away from this sacred place.

Children of the Clouds

The morning sky is bruised, and my children,
bright with noise, sitting on the front seat,
heading toward school, name the shapes
of the clouds: weasel, rooster, monkey, bee.
Even a dead squirrel smears the sky's asphalt.
Far off west, a black wall flattens hills.
What my children have not seen yet is the air's dancing heart,
the heart's light, its pulse and beat, its blood.
Thunder has not reached our carousing ears,
pregnant with the names of fat animals:
pig and hippo, elephant with tuba nose.
Rotund laughter crowds the embryonic car
until we arrive at the sterile school
where the kids are born into alphabet soup,
a curriculum of building blocks and library cards.
No sooner are they in the building than the water breaks.
The sky crowns, and the first raindrop of months
bawls upon the window its shock of entry.
A new season where none has been commences.
Streets dance with happy-hoofed children.
Children smile and laugh upon the windshield
and the abusive wipers cannot slap the joy away.

Self-Portrait

Here's a man bearing great weight.
Notice how the shoulders slide and sink,
how the back rolls, as maybe
a support collapses and his height
avalanches an inch.
He carries a small chest,
one so narrow
you'd sooner snap it
like a twig than hold it long—
he is no stick to walk with.
Was a time his belly was flat,
but paunched now,
the weight silts to the bottom
of his stomach's lake.
His legs are serviceable, though stilts.
His arms, his hands, his feet,
his tubular neck, leftover parts.
You can see his face sag,
around those tired-green eyes,
at his lips, that drawn purse.
His beard is dirty water,
and just beneath
the white trough along the curb.
His hair, loose, runs all directions.
It can't get far enough away.

The Yawn

In the beginning was the yawn. The woman sat reading
some old book on old literature, the lamp
a yellow fog behind her, the cat and the litter
sucking at her on the rug in front of the fireplace
of the television, the room hot with a bleeding
October. Rain had fallen all morning, stopped, and wind
mounted, leaves chatty as kids on the bed,
school the next day. Slowly the pages turned,
the eyes strained against sleep. She read the old
book, and in her mind—what might be there behind
the silence? Not the book, not that. Not
the cats or t.v., but maybe just silence.
She couldn't fight if she stayed quiet. She wouldn't
have to face the pain of the mistake. Don't speak,
don't give any reason for language. And yet the
yawn, the beginning, and yawn, the end of quiet.

The Big Empty

Even when birds flew overhead,
she could not permit joy.
Honkers and criers, wings broad,
affixed on crosswinds,
and she was full of their longing.

Somehow she saw the migration as emptiness,
the flatland a flat line. Her heart beat,
as wings do, but if she cried unfathomable bubbles
she heard it as needful music,
the tone and gong that knelled nothing.

Geese, ducks, crane—all accustomed to season,
were perverse, stuck in standstill,
going and coming, cutting cold and darkness—
they did not arrive; destination was always
past the next horizon, the next sunrise.

In the territory of no-progress,
the bankrupt heart felt freeze was absence of feeling;
in snow and wind, the long moan meant only mean misery.
In rain or drought, the place gasped.
Trees begged green; the dry bed,

the shallow stream of creek or air,
while they had carved, would carve permanence—
all evidence of dying, not of life.
All dead. So many ways to suffocate.
How much I tried to explain. Choruses

sang to her, as to all. The dome lit as much
as not, even *not* was something to adore
in silence, in patience. The time and place.

Split, 1992

Silence after—the car's hum,
making distance, a lullaby.
He sits in the old blue rocker,
one lone spring ticking like a clock
as the night whirls about him
and his babies. The walls of the house
are comfort, calm and plain,
photos that had hung there
tilted in boxes. She will be back. She will
be back. The kids asleep,
the snoring chair. He hopes otherwise.

Planning the Affair

Let me find her at noon,
at a fountain near a bank,
chewing on a burger.
Let me say something suave, like,
"Nice teeth" or "I have gum."
We'll skip work and wander aimlessly.
Talk about baseball. Or popcorn.
Or panhandle outside a theater.

Maybe we can drive to the country,
park in a pasture
with cows mooing at the windows.
Or lie beside a croaking pond.
Should the weather turn cool,
we'll rush to a sun-flooded room.

Why should it ever be dark?
Why bars and drinks and apartments
furnished with shadows?
Let every wrinkle or scar,
every stretch of belly,
flaw of breast,
sag of gut, ball, or butt,
be part of our blemish.

Let there be light
to celebrate the body's decadence.

Let the public be informed.

Custody

The man drove away slowly, his children
filling his rearview mirror. The daughter,
tall for her age, waved and waved and waved.
And the man had hoped to see her frown,
as if the motion of arm and hand were a wiper
on a windshield, slapping off the sky.
But everything was in reverse—
she smiled, happier than he wanted.
But the mirror distorts like a mind does.

The older son made his way up the stairs
that led to his mother's apartment. He had not looked back.
What could this mean? The stairs
should have been impossible—a mountain, craggy
and slippery. The man should have been there
at the mountain's bottom to catch the boy
who kept climbing, looking upward,
making his way to the cave of himself.

The younger boy leaped off the bottom step
and, the man thought, went running toward the car.
The boy's mouth was open, and the man heard,
beyond the engine's noise
and the doo-da of the radio, his son's voice
calling him back. *Stop, Daddy, stop,*
that voice called. It was the voice the small one
had used when his father had come into his room
to scare the ghosts away so that he could sleep.

How long ago had that been? Years, already.
The man stopped, put the car into reverse,
and backed. *What is it?* the man asked.

The son, perplexed, explained he was only running
to the neighbor's house to play.
It was well, then. Well. Well—then.

The man drove to the exit of the apartment complex,
past wrought iron gates suspended
from brick pedestals. A wicked turn left,
a knoll, and, as way leads to way,
the knoll lifted him up, let him down,
and the complex disappeared.

The Last Night

The night before I left to find some quiet,
to hear the voice of my soul and know
the direction it would choose for me to go,
we lay wrapped in each other's arms, entwined
and clothed in naked hope, washed in candlelight.

I spoke to her about the book we would write,
Two Swans, poems about our ringed flight.
I said we should have a photo shot to adorn the cover,
her bare breasts against my bare chest, lover to lover,
her hair veiling her face, my head turned down to hers—

soft and grainy, near dissolve, black and white
as if the bedroom's shadows lay over us.
I bathed her with kisses after that, a wash
of damp leaves falling from an autumnal tree, lush
layerings foot to head, front to back. All the while,

the deep, sweet lawn of her moved to the wind
my mouth made. The leaves pitched about,
the lawn dampened. Then, our sleep came, kind
and mindless, and too soon the unkind hour
when I would have to leave. Over coffeee, we talked—

I spoke my fears and then reaffirmed the bonds
we had made with each other, for there inside my soul
were all our coupled truths. I needed nothing more,
except put things to order. When I left, long
farewell in the kitchen, a few leaves more,

I trusted the wind, the leaves, the lawn,
saw our communal dissolve adorn life's long book,

and knew return was day after night, a turn
of the seasonal clock. Something so secure that shock
of any weather could not break the sacred hoop.

VI.

Montage

In Hitchcock's *Psycho*, Miss Crane informs Norman Bates
she's seeking a private island; he tells her a mother
is a boy's best friend. She doesn't mention
she's stolen 40,000 dollars and needs a place to hide,
though, even temporarily, a roadside dive like Bates Motel
will do. Norman omits he hides inside his mother's wicked bones.
They sit and smile shyly. How well deception bodes them:
one near redemption, the other hopeless.
She will say goodnight, soon—permanently, as she showers
and Norman arrives with knife in hand.
The bath spins a whirlpool down the drain,
the shower curtain and its rings liberate from the rod,
and the agonizingly delicate hands clutch the fabric
the way we might have wished she had held our hands
had she not given over to other affections.
Did Norman notice as we did, shackled to our seats?
Hitchcock understood the island afloat inside our crippled hearts,
stranded as we are in wheel chairs, watching out windows
while deranged neighborhoods strangle and stab each other.
Wanting to run, fearing the push from a cliff,
we imagine the private place as something special,
a berth on a train where newlyweds couple in the tunnel's dark
while we pass through the mountains slabbed over us.

Who knew it could be so dangerous, even in poetry?
Tennyson's Lady incarcerated, weaving images
of a world too evil to encounter; gay Lancelot loitering
on his handsome horse's back, the shine that tin
may bear under bright light. She is cursed for wanting
        the narcissistic man;
removed from her lonely, towered island she is just
a pretty face. Her songs fade, as well her seductive mystery.

Even romantic Coleridge, his new bride dumping boiled milk
upon his foot, transports from the lime-tree bower
he calls *prison*. The Kubla's icy dome melts to voices
that scrutinize and disapprove. A common practice
for verse and, worse, life itself: the island imagined
cannot forestall intrusions. Yeats, brooding
in a London flat, politics and state heavy on his mind,
disastrous love occupying his heart, longs Innisfree,
the bees in flowers, the noisy bugs and birds.
Disappointments wearing his soul shell thin,
is it no surprise he equates *glad* with *glade*?
Grey stones beneath his feet, he invokes the island and goes,
but history shows he never stays. He never really went.

What to do, then, when hurt looms like Rushmore noses
or crop dusters bomb us with DDT on country intersections,
and farm trucks loaded with melons collide with fiery catastrophe?
Imagine a creek, copper green, so narrow
you might step across, bank to bank, and not get wet.
Petrified wood, fossil shards—bones and teeth—
and Indian points little currents kick aside upon gray-ash beaches.
Prickly pear and yucca bloom and dragonflies
sending forth their squadrons like World War I biplanes.
Or the backyard where fall wind cools, jack pine and oak,
the scrubby bunch of green and yellow that sings
like papers crumpled when writing goes wrong.
The pattern's clear and lessons come nearly too late to do us good,
like Stewart in *Vertigo*, dangling from a gutter.
We prophesy our saving grace and hope *Grace* is more
than just a name.
Lest we fall. Though we fall. The testament
of discontinuance rides skiffs toward shallow Camelot.
Kettles on the boil always, fountains in windows,
rags and ravings, and decrees evaporated before dew can form.

Love sinks into Bates's backyard bog. But go.
Go to spite the spite, as showers steam,
as holes are dug from which we cannot rise,
as we slide off the faces of our forefathers.
Hopeless and one minute to redemption, go. Go now.

The Poets

How unhappy poets are:

Sylvia, her head in the oven,
cooking a roast for scholar-jews
who tinker on her fat-watch heart.

Or Anne, dragging on car exhaust
like a cigarette. Bad weather between lovers,
want of love was wanting to die.

Or Weldon, his words and paints put up,
no more jazz, no more cracks in the wall,
poised like a magician, Abracadabra, on the bridge rail.

And wild Dylan, drinking sun under the table—
I hear his rage, having also kissed
the lips of many bottles

and sucked their brown tits dry.
Morning-bitch boots my gut
with sun-heavy shoes; day thirsts

and deserts sit in my bony mouth
as word-dunes shift through my skull's bowels.
Every word a bullet, every line a neck-tie.

Poets merit hazard pay:
suicide sits naked and horny on their laps,
groping them.

Readers, having watched poets
barrel over falls,

think how weird *they* are.
Have they not tasted gunpowder
nor breathed gas,
nor loved the warmth of wrist-blood?

Among high limbs of impossible trees,
angst-birds throat death songs.
They listen, afraid to sing.

Little Sahara

The sun's light pierces the black panes
of the chrome and glass mountain, flooding the office,
swims rivers of ink that slip and course
among pyramids of daily ledgers and invoices,
warms its yellow coils on margins of papers,
basks there, then slithers over mail trays.
The little egyptian at his gray desk, at his gray task,
praying to the single eye of the Sphinx on the wall,
carves his Pharaoh's red and black hieroglyphy,
a holy work, a woeful work of Ages.
But the egyptian presses to his broad, pale forehead
a troubled hand. Locked in his mind's eye
is a vision of an oasis, of square islands and gardens,
of trees and of fruit sweet to the parched tongue.
There, his children dance in the fountain's mist
and rainbow, the sprinkler's folding and unfolding arch.
The sacrificed calf cooks on a black grid
over red, hissing coals; the cold tea
of the sun sweats Niles down the sides of his glass.

A phone rings and wakes him. A new epidemic,
a new burden and plague commences. The dream
dissipates like a mirage. The desk is a vast desert.
Like a nomad, he plods through endless dunes
of triplicate forms and letterheads.
Motes ascend the sun's bright bridge
and vanish into heaven's black, opaque glass.
Winds rise; the sand pelts the nomad's back.
He must keep moving or be lost, forever.

The Company Representative and the Trainee

Rain-smeared road. A shrill, knocking wind
where the hills open. Or close.
Slap of wipers and radio's sweet static.
Hum of tires, hum of tired man.

You expected something more?
Starlight's glow? Annunciation?
Friend, call me Heretic.
Night-crossing a desert of corn,
the only lights are the winking eyes of cats and coons,
or the haunted crypts some call homes.
Nothing else but grip of muscle, ache of bone.
Then infinite numbness.
This, the condition of the world.

Search for a quick profit,
a place to stop like an electric oasis
with soft beds and clean sheets,
sweet-smelling women nearby,
and stout coffee in a dull café.
Or, a friendly lounge
where they'll honor a travel-battered guest.

Stop thumping my door, Gideon.
Buy me a drink or let me sleep
until that bastard sun rises, again.

The Death of the Vaudevillian

Friends surround his bed. A magician
in a far corner pitches cards
at his top hat; in a vase on a desk
sit the flowers he pulled from his sleeve.

A little girl with a head of curls
does the soft-shoe. Only mother
applauds the act. "The Good Ship
Lollipop" swamps in solemnity.

For each minute he lives, a stripper
pulls off another long glove.
To the beat of life-support,
she bumps and grinds. What shtick!

A straight man tells him
an old joke: "A fella tells me
he knew a man with a wooden leg
named Smith. I asked him,

'What's the name of the other leg?'"
A big-boobed blonde in a nurse's cap
cries, "Doctor! Doctor!"
The vaudevillian doesn't respond. He

readies himself for a final performance.
A Great Curtain rises. Applause
thunders, horns and drums howl.
The top bananas take the stage.

Ah, yes: W. C. Fields juggling,
Ray Bolger dancing, and all

in red with red boa, Gypsy
Rose Lee. The drum:

bump-bump, bump-bump, bump-bump.
Pies and comics and nameless girls
in feathery costumes. The drums
roll, the cymbals of paradise clash.

Suddenly, his turn in the spotlight.
His big break, his punch line.
Timing. The timing must be perfect.
"Take my wife. Please."

Liberace in Heaven

for Jonathan Holden

The Glitter Palace! Streets of silver,
cream-smooth columns of burnished ivory.
The blinding gold of ten million candles topped
with celestial fire. Tenor choir
and rhapsody of scintillating music.
Tambourine jazz; satin-soft waltzes
and symphonies. God love those strings!
His kind of gig, the fanfare, glitz:
Las Vegas in the clouds. Simply too lovely,
and sweet, perfect androgyny: cherubs
and seraphim, soft-cheeked fellows,
and Peter, his best boy. Now, above,
the Pearly Gates swing. And still he gushes:
"Thank you. Thank you very much."

The Poem

The Poem expects to be important,
to be immortalized in fat anthologies,
bought by students who cannot comprehend genius.

The Poem will arise from its white tomb
like Lazarus, wrapped in ink's black cloak,
made perfect and inspiring awe.

The Poem will win the Pulitzer and Guggenheim,
reside in *Poetry* and *The New Yorker.*
Its yacht will ride the waves of Public Radio.

Great Poets will pay The Poem homage,
like Magi pursuing its uncontrollable mystery.
No matter that all Great Poets are dead.

It will win an NEA Fellowship, give readings
in exotic places, hold a Breadloaf.
Its praise will haunt the Library of Congress.

Like all great poems, The Poem
will bury its poet in a pauper's grave.
We who read it will not miss the poet.

Lesser poems languish in the absence
of their life-breathing demigods.
Bald heads murder them in seminar dissection.

But The Poem is naïve: it still believes
poetry makes things happen.
The dissatisfied poet tears The Poem up.
The sonuvabitch is going nowhere.

Digging for Fossils

And then you come face to face with it,
some wide-eyed fish stuck in stone
surprised to find you there in his ocean,
shocked at the light that never disturbed him
even as he lived.
And you can't begin to find words enough
to explain the value of this meeting.
You try, but all that comes from your throat
are little chipping sounds like a chisel and hammer
tapping at the rock.

And maybe it's predictable.
But later, when you crawl into your tent to sleep,
and mosquitoes buzz about your head like sand
silting to a lake's bottom,
you hear the same chipping sound,
you open your eyes in surprise at the light
washing in eons around you,
then surprise again when you see the bright blue eyes
of someone looking at you, tape in hand
to measure your occipital, the jut of your jaw,
the distance between the centers of your eye sockets.
You hear the low sound of her voice speaking a language
that sounds like metal against rock,
and you're wanting to tell her what it is
you could tell her.

The Lie

could not wait to rush out the front door,
scurry down broken sidewalks to the neighbor's place,
instigate play, and please herself in the mischief
she concocted. Tall tales were like tall trees to climb,
branches sweeping down webs of clouds,
piracies to wage against heavy ships
that could not swim swiftly enough to evade engagement.
No matter that the neighbor kids always ran home,
bruised or bloodied, dirt streaking their faces.
Words are clods, snowballs with rocks at their centers.
She loved drama—her backyard the entire town,
the leaves and blossoms of the forsythia everyone's attention.
Her dogs barked loudest of all dogs, and in the clubhouse
of her heart were the repetitive notes of hammering.
No telling what she was building; she was always
building. Sometimes she wearied of the effort,
and feigning sleep, she might shed a snore, snort a tear.
She loved most a lullaby wrought by violins or violence—
she couldn't tell which (to sound the same is to be the same).
Metonymy of worries worried into realities.
If kids she bullied no longer wished for fist or untruth's boot,
she did not care. Always others to run to, ears big as buckets.

The Brain-Eaters

The natives, first, unbudded themselves,
seemed beautiful and fresh,
unblemished by paint or wardrobe.
The way through the jungle had been miserable:
heart-sweat bore the man down,
and heat locked up his brain.

For days and nights the natives danced
around him, gleeful and cheery.
Fed him full with roots of love,
fruits of passion, meat of hope
which he had lost somewhere in undergrowth
of coiling vine and cutting leaf.

They kept him awake and would not let him sleep.
He took this as part of the ceremony.
But—he became numb, and that was when
they cut open the bulb of his skull
and dipped their fingers into his brains
and licked the stringy frosting.

When the skull was scooped out,
they packed in straw and roly-poly bugs,
put the scalp-cap back on and sewed it shut.
Whenever he thought about pain,
the straws crackled and he forgot.
Whenever he hurt, the roly-poly bugs tucked.

He began to take comfort in this existence.
There was a dull pleasure in the squawk of jungle bird
or in the whistle of the color yellow
as it slipped along the backs of snakes

that sunned upon creek-side stones.
The natives danced, always, and his eyes danced.

Yet—a yearning sat in his center, a throb
that seemed a music from a time long-past.
He asked the natives if they might not eat his heart.
The natives refused, and some, offended,
ran into the black foliage, screaming.
The whole jungle raged.

What does this mean? he asked the healer.
Why would they not eat my heart?

It is poison, the healer answered,
and we do not care to die.

Surviving

It's like a moving man who isn't paid enough
to move the expensive, delicate crystal,

carefully packing each glass baby
into a crib of bubble wrap and laying it sacredly

into the heavy pasteboard box, folding
the flaps down as one would tuck a blanket.

Or the tape going on, like a priest doing something holy,
the way the hands move, exorcising.

All the way to the new destination, the City of Peace,
his slow truck taking centuries,

every bump missed. You'd expect he'd throw
the stuff together, to trip on the loading ramp,

to send the glass careening to the pavement.
All those beautiful tumblers, those long-stemmed roses

of precious ice. Sweet Jesus, how shattered stars shine!
He's not paid enough to struggle with the chore,

yet he does, singing lullabies. The slick ramp,
pavement a fall away, isn't at all slippery.

Accidents just don't happen. One foot carefully
in front of the other, shoestrings immaculately tied,

the moving man breathes easily and hefts
the crystalline weight.

Perhaps he has angels in overalls
to sweep away tripping stones.

Perhaps we're with him and our fragile parcels,
on our hands and knees,

making our silent, tearful supplications,
whisking obstructions into hungry palms.

So happy to help.

The Heart

The heart stands on her corner beneath a lamp
so dim the passersby, cozy in their own darkness, almost
fail to notice the tragic plunge of cleavage,
the red satin mini and fishnet hose.
Put a smoke in her permanent pout, a glaze
in her eyes, she'd be one of those lost ladies,
pretty party for a price. That's what they think,
so, shamed, they duck their heads and pace faster.
The heart hurts, of course.
The night upon her, no one there for her, stood up,
an emptiness comprised of bankrupt-need, she watches
traffic ease past to turn corners,
near misses of intersections, hears bleating horns
that sing *Come along*, or curse, *Hurry up*
through the flat, dismal rain.

Death's Door

Finding yourself at Death's door
is like driving through a pleasant countryside,
all hills and valleys, pitch of steep,
pit of river, the end of vacation.
It's the piddling up and down elm-lined streets
of a small town, the middle-class panorama.
Green lawns and pregnant trashcans at the curbs
awaiting delivery. We never know which house
is Death's, exactly, nor which driveway
will lure us in. We never know, until, like epiphany,
the door we can't resist appears,
and it's a short walk up a stone path,
flower plots filled with lilies of the valley and jonquils;
a blue spruce looming above the front stoop,
needles red and brown like a carpet
where the grass should grow were there sun,
were there more than the gray dust that drought
has laid there. The porch wears recent paint,
but beneath the new enamel old regrets flake
or bear the scars of someone
who tried to scrape them smooth.
A porch swing but Death doesn't swing.
Wicker furniture for hot summer days,
a glass of tea or red wine,
but Death stays cool inside the house, in shadows,
awaiting the visitor who comes to poke
the doorbell with painful inquisition.

Were it not for the busybodies, Death would read
last words from whatever lost books
he found on his shelves. He would eat
whatever last supper fit his plate.

He would nap and prepare.
The visitors all want to see what he's done with the house.
Come on in, Death says, *let me make you feel at home.*

The Intercessor

Sometimes I am certain the only one
who prays for me is me, the solicitor

having been turned from the doors
of friends and family, none willing to buy a token.

He used to come in and sit at the table,
its cloth white and lacey, and unfolded

the many compartments of his valise,
spilling out the miracles that might quickly

open a can of worms or dice up our salad lives,
trinkets and gadgets whose value we believed in

and bought though our pockets were empty.
I saw him, walking away, down the heavy sidewalk

beneath willows bowing as he passed,
elms that rained tears and bugs screwing haloes

onto street lamps. These days, he wipes clean
the windshields of cars paused at stoplights,

intersections filthy with hurry, faith a dollar bill
so long as the light is red. Somehow,

I believe in the magic valise more than
the necessity of a clean window.

The greatest poverty may be only
that I am he who prays for himself,

maybe down on my luck, down to my last dime
or my last dime spent over and over,

electricity at home disconnected.
I'm prepared for a knock on the door,

to slip the smiling man all my change
through the crack of a car window,

his squeegee in hand, mean traffic around us.

Weldon Kees at the Bridge

"This ghost of yours, padding about . . . ."

If Weldon leapt—and surely he did—magic
held him briefly aloft, Bay wind surrounding
him like angels, merciful at last. The tragic
plunge—the spiraling, twisting, confounding
his senses—was not merely a fall to dark water.
He'd done that already, possessing it as he could,
locked inside his poems. What had any of it mattered?
Picture him falling, happy at last, his indisputable mood
a giddy hilarity. Perhaps he lost his breath,
his consciousness before collision. Perhaps he felt no pain,
only something drunken and amazing: death
sweeter than he had hoped for. He was Icarus, his gain
the puzzling disappearance; his words, for my life,
imperishable. A hocus-pocus in the magician's flight.

The Uptown Bar

for Larry Holland

A bottle of Yukon Jack sits on an old oak table,
the cowboy's hat tipped low over his eyes,
but God's eyes fiercely drunk, his tongue animate.

I made this table, God brags, and this drink, too.
The cowboy nods, Yessir, but what oak woods
have you walked recently, and how often

do you have a friend to drink and shoot shit with?
I made the horses, God adds, wincing—the shot is stout,
and the cowboy says, When was it you last rode one?

So how was it there? God wonders. The cowboy smiles:
A wet line, a drawn bead, dew at morning camp.
Place enough, and enough in place.

All your works, God, good.
I had me a devil of a fine time.

VII.

Pancakes

The pancakes we tossed upon the garden plot,
batter-mushrooms on compost flat,
have flown away in the beaks of blue jays.
The birds were laughing there,
glad beggars breaking bread,
while a dove prayed like a brown-cloaked monk
and drank his communal wine
beneath a leaky garden spigot.

At the window, parting a sink-sea of suds,
we watched the manna pilgrims come in separate homage,
squirrel and cat, rat and crow,
nervous as they stalked the rubbish we left.
The hopeful hungry in the place of plenty.
Then made them flee, when, as from behind heaven's veil,
we opened a door and banished them from backyard Eden,
and did so because, as gods, we could.

The Cranes, Texas January

I call my wife outdoors to have her listen,
to turn her ears upward, beyond the cloud-veiled
sky where the moon dances thin light,
to tell her, "Don't hear the cars on the freeway—

it's not the truck-rumble. It is and is not
the sirens." She stands there, on deck
a rocking boat, wanting to please the captain
who would have her hear the inaudible.

Her eyes, so blue the day sky is envious,
fix blackly on me, her mouth poised on question
like a stone. But, she hears, after all.
January on the Gulf,
warm wind washing over us,
we stand chilled in the winter of those voices.

My Children's Inheritance

Every father leaves his children and resents
his leaving. Which is it?: the ice that touches
the pond's edge and retracts and only the hint
of coldness remains. Or: heat leaves
on the backs of crane and snow geese,
and cold stays. One of these legacies
I leave my children whose father-image
fades with each new, bright daylight.
Or: the cold dissolves in their rain.
Today, though, a thousand thousand
leaves leapt from their branches,
and having done so, kept trying to leap
from the ground they committed themselves to.
They could not escape—each roll and twist
tumbled down road or sidewalk. I could hear their
mumbling, *sorry, sorry, sorry.*

Talking November Weather, Long Distance

Again, across the miles, my mother's voice
is optic thin. Are you sick, I ask. *The weather,*
she says, *so hot one day, cold the next.*
The wind will not stop blowing and there's dust
and mold in the air. Not just her,
she tells, but my sister and nephews have the illness, too,
getting over it, getting it back.
Isn't that the way the weather works,
moving from one extreme to the other?
I used to think so, but where I live
Texas heat is perpetual. My body rains.

We talk about my oldest sister's family,
the woman, who, angry at cancer, connected
disease to my divorce and refused to death to speak.
Have you heard from any of them, I question.
No, no, nothing. It's hard for them,
now she's gone. But, I remind her,
life was hard when she was here, for everyone.
Yes, yes, that's true. The weatherman says
the snow will fall deep. I may have to shovel.
Can't you find someone to do that for you?
I know I'm wasting air. She's 82,
her body like a piece of lattice.
Mom, if you fall, you may find it difficult to get back up.
O, we all get back up until it's time not to.
Then someone else can breathe the dust
we used to breathe, shovel the snow
we no longer feel the weight of.

For Travis, Disappointed by First Love

Where does the bird fly once it leaps?
Somewhere past its own melody,
the old wood of fence post smooth as absence,
strand of wire the heart's barbed-tension.

What is the sound of what was once its song?
The beautiful, most painful silence of the world:
the frozen snowdrift, the brown leaf
wedged inside a window's screen,
the impossible entry inescapable.
That, and all that might be imagined in such silence.

Who must remember the music made more than music?
It must be you. Inside the circle of one
there is just the one memory
and the one dependence.
Innuendo the breathing after the note.

When might wings find their wind-felt ways back?
Seasonally. Every warmth has its chill.
Every migration its night-journey back.
The sun dance among gold reeds.

Will it be the same?
All alters. Even stones change.
But the spirit of bird is an emotion
as antique as its liquid word.

Why must the bird fly?
All of life is cage.
The leap a wonderful, horrible freedom.
The disappearance at horizon an entry.

Were it anything else, it would not be bird.

How will you survive?
As we all must, our ears open for the next sensation
of continued song.
You can hear it, just beyond sight.
Just beyond hold.

Syllogism: On Highway 12, Clearwater River

Clouds hung like gauze canopies
halfway up the Bitterroot foothills;
white pine like shadowed men
hiked the sure steps to heaven
that lay just beyond the wisp-dimmed summits.
It rained all morning.

I picked up pinecones
that later did not make the airplane home,
the Clearwater's white roil a toe, a slip away.
I've read how pinecones
cannot seed except by flame,
the forest on fire—that things destroyed
replenish. A man is pinecone, too.

Thus, pinecones that day rode aluminum boats
and cast lines into the river—
fish, all alive, all new, all wild and sparked with light
they swam too deep to see,
hung flapping on stringers, the pinecones smiling.
And pinecones on horseback dared the rocky escarpments.
Or drank Alaskan ale at Hogan's Bar
across the blue bridge in Washington
and wondered if they should go home at all.
Fire comes in more ways than one.
Ash to tree, ash to man.

My Son, at Post, Camp Victory, Baghdad

The soldier stands guard on the tower,
razor-wire coiled atop chain link
that constitutes his perimeter.
The coils remind him of springs
inside the mattress he and his buddies
used in backyard wrestling matches—
Marc Marvel versus Voodoo—
until the mattress popped
and foam inside spilled
its politics.
The comparison strikes him as funny,
and though it's the middle of the night,
he suppresses an urge to grin. He's tired,
he knows it, but darkness has an edge
that ribbons rest. He must stand attentive.
Gun noise and blasts
sound, because of distance,
like fireworks at a Fourth of July celebration
in a little Nebraska town,
a civilized square compressed
in the orbit of wheat or corn fields.
The spray of rockets, embers gold and green and orange,
are the umbrellas of weeping willows
over park lawns,
and the picnic and ball game noise
seems thick as gunpowder smoke.

The ghost-hour come around again,
he watches for what is not there
to see if the darkness watches back.
It's not nervousness;
it's not that there are hours left

before day breaks
its shell and the sun oozes yolk.
It's not even absence of conversation.
The haunting that arrests his heart
is knowing, after sleep,
the little town
will be this desert place instead,
filled with the language
of misunderstanding, of doubt, of need.
Better to wake to the tune of wind in elms,
lumber creaking in old rafters,
warm air sifting
through window screens and feeling cool as water;
to step from bed and out the door
to an old bike and throw papers
to neighbors whose eyes speak all you need to know.

This is the territory to go to,
the hard choice of shoes or bare feet,
the only land foreign
being that place
we would never dream of going.
The only war worth fighting.

Anxiety

sleeps on the steep rooftop while carpenters
slap shingles into place, the noise like machine guns
and woodpeckers. Pneumatic drills
plug holes through asphalt as hot-mix trucks
dump their landslide sludge. Nearby, kids leap from the high board
at the neighborhood pool and spank hard their silly asses.
A three-story drop through air's sleeve
of elm leaves and black limbs is always
just a gasping inch away, the water as hard as the ground.
Let collapse of structure—roofs and walls—stop.
Make gravity fail. Let blessings be breeze when sun sears;
let sun's sear quench the chill skating the skin's glacial plain. Calm
would be miracle rain as dust awaits stirring.
But, the road maintained
maintains old indentations; the pothole will be driven into,
and the jolt is the thick advent of storm,
bolt and pummel of thunder like the turning
of an unexpected corner into an unfamiliar neighborhood.
Every neighborhood is unfamiliar. Strangers
behind broken fences and rusted trucks bark and bray.
Composites stick. Soap or solvent cannot strip the grime clear.
Worry a wall walked into, an intruder on every porch,
the heart is a door broken through, all alarms concerted.

New York, January 2007

My wife and I stand on the 58th Street subway platform,
awaiting the Soho train. Her hair, wet from rain,
spills from beneath the hood of the sweatshirt
she wears back West riding a horse or brushing out its mane.
Three days unshaven, I'm equally soaked, our umbrella
broken from midtown wind. Still on Pacific time,
eyes heavy and dreary as Idaho's winter, a hardness
we bear must seem city. Tourists, thick with accents
and apprehension, clueless, approach and ask:
Is this the train to the Battery? Is this going to the Village?
We help as we can, pointing out numbers
and letters on a Metro map, wish them luck and let them go.
The trains' doors are insatiable and eat what we offer,
people with cameras and baggage and valises full
of papers for meetings. When they return home,
perhaps they'll speak of hospitable cliff-dwellers,
roosting among skyscrapers instead of mountains,
the high desert less about topography than attitude.
Meanwhile, we navigate Manhattan, visit
with old men walking fat dogs, restaurant owners
about knish and matzo balls, barter with dealers
of hotdogs and knock-off handbags,
and eat Reubens and bagels and lox among hardhats.
Just once, when a man asks where the post office is,
we disappoint: *We're not from this part of town.*
He looks over the top of foggy glasses, one hand
clutching an envelope, the other palm upward,
a panhandler catching dimes of rain.

On Horseback,
Hell's Gate Canyon, October

for Kimberly

We ride past basalt columns, ascend
a cow face to top an outcropping
above the Snake and sit there, and watch.

Here is the topography of desire: a sky heavy
with grey smoke, the blue and ancient river,
unrequited; the rogue, stiff bunch

of thistle and sage, brown, curled coneflowers,
and across the stream the accumulated green.
All those oppositions that pull toward a center.

Like the pleated hills of the canyon, distance
pushes away, pushes past an irreparable edge.
Yet here we are, two long-time lovers on horseback,

relics to a belief, putting the pieces together
that creation could not. Constancy a thing
like a slow horse plodding along the veins

that bighorn and cattle cut through rock.
Trust like giving the horse his head
to feel his way over stony rubble,

perilous going, getting there.

VIII.

The Fiction of Place

stumbles,
old heavy horse, upon a motion
that creates more motion:
physics of dust and noise, things drawing near
or away. Beneath the clop
of hooves on clods, the place
really is just, after all, a place.
It is the story you hear and believe

and choose to love on your sickbed—
sleepless, aching, feverish—
desiring wellness and the place to find it.
Locale and its lies
delude to comfort you.
Should you rise
to run or walk
through snow or rain—

which accentuates a phrase
or clause—wind wailing,
hoarfrost graying
elms or maples, the fencerow planks,
or, if in sun, to toast
like gamma grass or some reedy,
heavy-headed stalk of weed,
a stemmy silence

allures you. Below the frost line
of your heart's hope,
place cares nothing
for you. How many love affairs
have you had, what
will convince you of your lovelessness?

How often do you part the curtains
    of a wintry morning,

watch cardinals and sparrows
    dance among drifts and squalls,
sheltered behind gray trunks
    to peck at seed
to feed their puny little lives,
    their puny little appetites
with puny little, and you say,
    God bless this place?

or some little nothing
    equally little and nothing?
Place does not love back,
    wants only your ill need
to give yourself away to it.
    The failure of poets
is their insistence to love
    what will not reciprocate.

Better to ride a clumsy horse
    down a rocky slope, tumble, fall,
crash. Better to let the beast
    breathe heavy, bone protruding
from a leg, the horse's scream
    the wind cannot diminish.
Forget that
    you lie under the animal,

its whole broken weight
    upon your leg, your chest.
You will both die here; it will be unpleasant.
    There is no point to love place.

*

So, when asked, write it like this:

Once a man walked out into the subzero—
winds, sleet and ice.
His eyes teared, and tears froze
in little rivulets upon his wind-burned cheeks.
His lungs ached hollow.
Snow crunched
and accepted his weight,
the ice beneath toughened his balance.

Chores: hay to buck
and feed, thick and dusty
in the loft, where fifteen barn cats
in a felinial ball on an old horse blanket
hunkered warmth—in the snow
and lashing wind they would have died,
cold in their paws crippling them,
the coyotes, roaming in

from white-shocked hills
and the overgrowth of cedar shelter,
eating them. This is how
the wind felt to the man—it had teeth.
The slippery ground
was a trap to make him fall,
to hurt him, and, if circumstance allowed,
to kill him with sleep.

Landscape furled out all around him—
it might as well have been the ocean,
it's as easy to drown there.
He had counted how many hills
he could see from his back step so often
he no longer counted. He knew how many

steps to the barn, how many
to the grange, his arms loaded with horse hay.

The ledger was pointless and as red as his face.
The numbers never varied,
the trouble, the weight
of things he must carry that served
the things that carried him.
The horses stood in the middle
of the snow-swollen pasture,
grumbling, shawled with frost,

stamping hooves, locomotive steam
rising from portal nostrils.
He could never quite hurry enough.
They did not worry that he stumbled
in the ruts they gouged. They might choose
to be stubborn and not join up.
When the hay was dropped,
as if begrudgingly, they would eat.

*

This is how to write
the fiction of a place—aloof,
distant as horizon is distant,

always at the doorway
both entrance and exit,
cold in heart, cold in thought.
We carry what carries us,
and place—lives and stories
and myth aside, romance aside—
never noticing we were there,
carries us longer.

IX.

Conditions of Grace

The horse knows the peripheral like a fear—
a sudden leaf, the pheasant jumping with a shriek
from a thicket of thistle,
the vine that could be snake.

Shadow the ancient memory
of wolf, bear, cougar.

Rear. Turn. Run, tail raised like a flag,
and kick.

*

The girl who rode his back was a pleasure—
bearing no weight, she felt like flex of shoulder muscle,
the pushing flank.

She was horse as he was horse.
When she rode it was the way he galloped.

*

The rain fell all day on the horse
who stood beneath the leafless black oak.

He did not regret his predicament.

His flesh, beneath bay skin, trembled.

A beautiful day to stand, as oaks do,
and shine with wet.

*

The black mare wore a shawl of snow.
The snow fell, was going to fall, just as the night was obligated.

Bit by bit, the mare disappeared.
White washed over black, black over white.
Only she knew where she was.

*

The bay and sorrel carried their riders down a long path.
Side by side, heads lifting, dropping,
a constant music of hoof percussion.

Palisades of columnar lava formed cliffs.
Fescue and thistle, magpies and buntings,
made a leafy quiet.

*

The rope slashed at the mare's face and neck,
and though she tried to pull back
to escape the trainer's fury, the holler, boot, and strike,
the mare could not run,
could not rear,
could not turn to kick,
held as she was by the rope that beat her.

She failed and failed, no fight, no flight,
until, at last, the woman rode her wherever she wanted.

Alone, in her stall, there was peace again,
the broken ground beyond the paddock gentle.
But the horse was out of her, galloping somewhere,
over a knob.

*

When the one-eyed dog ran the field,
it ran between the legs of the horse.
Catching it, the horse rolled the dog
which yelped and limped behind the rider and the horse that
hurt it.

The dog knew to keep its distance.

The horse, though, never knew there had been a dog.
It was just one of many clods on a cloudy afternoon.

Why We Bought a Horse

After our boy died, the black mare
was necessary: bug-eyed, underfed,
ribs like lath. We didn't know
she was dangerous, her ears pinned flat
against her head as much a warning

as a red flag on a beach
where Portuguese men-of-war land
their flotilla, the diamondback's rattle,
or the siren's wail as clouds fold
and wind bucks rooftops off.

Necessary thing she was, we didn't know
wildness disapproves halter, lead, longe-line,
the coaxing regardless how gentle.
That first time, nylon rope melting calluses,
she reared to strike front hooves down.

I dodged the tumult, tried again, and,
next, was awarded the hip-pivot
to kick. Round and round, the mare
and I danced, one step from disaster,
one slip from what was paramount

for those closest to me, wishing death
upon themselves, desiring dust
beneath the horse's hooves. She
had stood her ground before against others.
Knowing enmity of unwant,

she worked death out of me.
Her stampings my heart's knocking,

her bolting as from invisible fear
my stubborn holding on. I stayed
with her, stayed with her,

stayed with her until she calmed
at my singing, until she plodded behind,
head down, hooves hoving quietly.
Until, among similar enemies,
wild things made peace.

The Idaho Farm, June 2004

Standing out behind the barn,
feeding seven horses, my wife says,
"This is our piece of ground.

This is our piece of ground!
What we worked for, all this dirt
and green, that sky, that blue

and green, all that sky, all those blues
we can finally let go." Good news
for now, hope like good news.

For now, hope like seven horses,
feeding, nodding, hooves solid.
Where they stand, we stand.

108°—The Horse Pasture

Morning's haze burns to deep blue.
The horses, leaving the lean-to's shade,
lumber toward the barn door, hooves
dragging powder, lifting dust that seems brown fog.

Hay that is hot is deepest sweet,
and the horses come abject and penitent
through the sun's brightness, the pasture
nubbed to cooked nothing,

toward the flakes I toss them. Dull green embers
fly back into my face, light upon my hair
and clothes. It's hay smoke I inhale,
hay burn I wear. The third week of dry, high desert,

mountain valley choked on smoke
from fires up the Clearwater. All things
particled, we breathe and toke the ash
of ourselves. I've come to an hour in life,

a quarter to death, and fever of climate
tells me it's good to languish in thick air,
to trod the sift we become. We graze
the furnace that brazes us,

stand immersed in weather intolerant
and bland, ourselves intolerant and bland,
going as horses go, seeking sweetness
and a shade to which we'll return.

Meteor Shower, and Horses

I stand in the middle of the horse pasture,
six geldings lolling around me,
the night sky riddled with bullets of light.
Look out, I say, *the stars are falling.*

Horses never look up but stare
at the ground, face assward chilled breezes.
They nod, not in approval, but as
trees do, in comfort from movement.

I stand in the middle of the horse pasture.
Sweet horse smell, grass and leather, bleeds
like the night sky, riddled with bullets of light.
The stars spin, the horses hover.

Were I the axis of the casual universe,
lord of ground or mood inside chilled breezes,
something not human, I'd do as horses do,
as trees do, taking comfort in motion

and in the mesmerizing harmony
of six geldings lolling around me,
chords of light streaking the sky.
Look out, I say, *the sky is falling.*

The horses do not look up. They stare
into an emptiness they care nothing about,
nod, not approving, but like
all the angels of the earth, wearing

hooves or standing on two legs.
Quiet giants have nothing to gain in black sky

riddled with bullets of light.
            Let all stars fall, the sky fall

near our faces, what is ahead is ahead.

The High Desert, Idaho, September

for Kimberly and Claire

The fox sat at the foot of a mudslide knob,
a gully's gash, washed by wind and water,
behind him. Dust had muffled the clop
and clip of hooves, and, if he was surprised,
he hid it with disinterest. He had not run
but stood motionless as basalt
and stared at the three of us on horseback.
We pulled up reins to watch and our geldings,
sensing what they had not seen,
flared their nostrils, snorted, pawed the sunburned dirt.

Cheat grass and yucca, blooms like white flags,
scarcely moved. The river in the valley beneath us
mirrored sky, and clouds, sedate and slow,
pushed on like horses heading home.

Physics

The horse would leap
when birds flew from tufted grass,
half turn a circle and bolt
down rock-sided trails.

The birds cut away in wide, prevailing arcs,
sweeping over switchbacks
and mudslide scabs
while the rider clung to the saddle horn,

knees locked, feet pressing
stirrups. Tension like a spring
near to breaking,
the causal universe,

once calm and inert,
snapped into motion.

Feeding Horses, During Snow

1

You walk out to the horses, pasture grass glazed,
 ice crunching underfoot, your arms loaded with hay.
The horses, cold. Backs and manes draped in white lace,
 they quiver and murmur at a far corner beneath two elms that,
  leafless,
provide only comfortable recollection of last summer.
 Wind pushes, nudges, spurs. See how it is:
the horses' heads bowed, bottom lips pouting,
 impatient hoof-stomp, neck-sway, the nostril-steam.

2

Snow's haze makes small even largest things: the barn reduced,
  the trees;
 gray dissolves distance between you and your neighbors.
Stands of aspen, twists of raspberry, a progress of fence rows—
  all diminish.
 You know yourself as the cold which strides to meet the horses
who, when wind began cooling, danced and tossed their heads,
 farted as they bolted, tails up, feeling good. Now the geldings
are spirits—you click your tongue to stir them,
 you summon their names loud and prayerfully.

3

This is how it is with them, white weight
 like horse knowledge. When they turn their heads,
nickering and sighing, puffing steam, they don't see you.

Not hear your boots cutting snow, breaking frozen grass,
not sense the layers that house the unfamiliar animal stalking their way,
not see your face, not you who blankets, saddles, cinches them,
bits them, rides them, but the hay they want,
the alfalfa heat, necessary and green.

Horses, Considering Winter

Once we stood beneath
bare elm branches
as drizzle fell;
hair, slick and hugging skin,
twitched like wind-teetered leaves.
Wet crawled over us
and seemed flies or gnats.

The night just before ice,
six sets of lights infused
the gravel road, motors
humming, droning, pebbles grinding;
tires slushed slop,
and the softness we heard there
was the cavity and the abscess coming.

The lights we dared
to be eyes of predators stalking
so we might run, might
fire the furnace that heats
a horse, that it might ease chill.
Sometimes a horse wishes to die
in the shadow of the rain's shadow,

body's steam like a soul leaving.
Beneath the elms, locked
as we were inside a square pen,
we might have found death warm.
A miserable time for horses:
November wet,
when it will not yet snow

and ice mats the mane,
hangs in tail-hair. We lower our heads,
abject; stand prayerfully
with half-closed eyes
though horses do not pray—
we understand that as human frailty.
Watch how it is,

how we shiver, paw, nicker,
to see how prayers of horses go.
Who knows as well as horses
that hell is not a place
of heat, where grassfires
burn pastures black?
Nor is it other than where we are now,

this cold place, this wet place,
this sometimes buried place
when snow finally erases us.
We know, too, that inside
the misery falling
there is proof of a heaven
for horses. Gospel in rain drops,

the hymn in hoof percussion,
the running across rough range.
As we were meant for.

Grace, This Spring

This morning, from my garden,
I watched the horses nub at new grass,
their eyes half-closed to the meager meal,
ears lobbed forward catching, no doubt,
the hums of neighborhood inferences—
saws and hammers, trucks straining,
cars in a hurry. These did not concern them.
The horses moved in singularity, in giant patience.

Much to be done, though: last year's squashes
dissolving in the garden, unpicked okra
on their stalks like horse ears, spent leaves
needing turned under. Something to repair.
A robin sat on the fence nearby;
we made our exclamations and rose to our work.

The Horse Considers Hell

Not heat nor flame, but blacktop drone—
trailer tires and endless miles,
wind whistling tenor madness, rain
pouring in, the pooling mist
that blooms upward from behind the truck.

In long night dreams, we might ascend
a switchback, endure a saddle
and the labor that sits there, top a slope
and see the valley unfurl, the breezy slip
of creek or river; might run a pasture,
spin, buck, fart, or stand beneath
a slanted roof as sleet bullets.
Prayer is
heads dropped forward, a back hoof
lifted in rest, sanctum beneath birch boughs
where leafy shadows, holy
and nothing less, wash away summer's rage.
This: how to go.

But tied and haltered, paneled off,
the haul unending, long heat, longer cold.
It is the heaviness we bear upon our hooves
and the heaviness we bear upon our hooves.

Nine Choruses, in Which Horses Play a Part

1.

In the morning, there was wind.
The horse's eyes half-closed against it,
the mane, pulled beyond the length of its strands,
the tail that tried to fly.
The horse stood there, as a hawk does, halted in air.

In the afternoon, there was wind.
The eyes half-closed.
The mane pulling, the tail.
The horse there still, the hawk, somewhere, there.

In the night, the wind.
The horse had not moved at all.
The wind and the hawk the air took away had a place to get to.
The horse, patient, persistent, did not.

2.

Climbing the cow face up the ridge,
the old gray leapt, leapt, leapt.
The hooves dug and kicked down rock.
The sky, cloud-mottled, bright with sun,
waited at the top.

Behind him, down basalt slopes,
a ribbon of river sparkled like the shine
on darkest grass.

The curious horse never saw that. On the way down,
he eyed the trail where his feet would land,
the ground more dangerous than the sky.

3.

How sweet the heads of coneflower.
How sweet the brome.
How sweet to feel firm earth underfoot, the dust lifting,
the music of chew, the rhythm of stomp.

4.

The yearling, driven by a man in a straw Bailey,
ran the round pen until she was breathless, sweaty, greasy.

The hooves drove up a dust that smelled like her.

Later she walked, on halter and lead,
behind the man, her head down.

Humbled, she had left her spirit driving the dust in the pen.

5.

The woman who fed the young paint apple treats
let the horse's lips quiver against her palm.
This was a closeness species could share—
morsel and kiss.

6.

The man hung to the gelding's neck,
rubbing the black luster, the strong jaw.
The man enjoyed and believed his horse did, too.

It was good to please the man.
The gelding wanted his alfalfa.
He could wait a while longer if he had to.

7.

The mare would not be ridden.
She would take the bridle, the blanket, the saddle,
the cinch, the back strap.
She would not take the rider.

Explode. That, she would do.
The fence rail, the ground, taking all her weight.
She dared the rider on. Pain was nothing.

Bred, though, her eyes softened.
The hand that scratched her withers, that left its impression
on her back, flank, hip, tummy, teats,
she accepted.
She'd follow that touch. Intention was everything.

8.

At first the water was cool to drink,
but the rider urged him into the creek.
The horse danced a little, feeling for surety,
light in the water like a million fireflies.

Then, feeling good, stepped sprightly.
The sun blanched, the air dry.

9.

The horse in the trailer saw, as best it could,
the blur of long miles, distant mountains
where white pine stood beneath snow-topped crags,
sheen of rivers, the monotony of posts.

Trucks and cars buzzed past. A familiar noise
the horse flipped its tail to, keeping flies off.

X.

Anecdote of the Horses

I took six horses to Texas,
turned them loose in a pasture
deep blue with coastal grass
filled with wind that bent the reeds.

I turned them from their trailer,
and they ran as herd in a wide wave
like geese that ride winter wind
or a surge that mounts a sandy beach.

They encompassed all that new space,
hooves rumbling like breakers,
the curving ebb of drawn-in tide.
But nothing like any water in Texas.

Early Morning on Farm Road

Deer lie down in coastal grass
where horses, knee-deep and dreaming,
stand and nod then face in slow wakefulness
the fog that drifts and blazes with first sun.
Yellow mist, gold haloes crowning oaks and ash.
Barbed-wire strums with whirrings
of wren and finch, such little wheels,
and the country road, under still heavy dew,
lulls like a snake, so chilled it cannot move.

In Hurricane, with Horses

The man, gray-flannel shirt lifted overhead
shielding him, strides long, alone in the blow—north
then south, cold then hot. Who would think
to count the rain, weightless, infinite, like slivers.

He yells and whistles silence against the howl
at six horses hunkered under oaks at pasture's end.
All around, the woods groan, their bones pop.
The sky churns blackening butter.

Waist-deep grass underfoot rolls flat
as by waves upon a long shore. A loblolly pine
collapses, its root ball like a molar;
a wire tangle blossoms barb and spark.

The horses circle upon the circle of themselves.
He stands at their nervous center, an eye. Easy now,
he coos, and slips the halter upon the oldest head,
the one to lead the rest to shelter.

Now unhurried nudge through rivers in air,
as in the plodding cadence of the high terrain,
the rocky switchback. Pitch and plunge
looming above them, clouds like cliffs ascend.

A Thousand Reasons

After rain, day's end, steam rises
from the pasture, coastal hay summer brittle.
Fog sits on the cool green of loblolly pine
and white oak. Egrets at a pond's edge
at the edge of sight lift and float away.
Twilight darkens.
                                        The old horse, retired,
sullen and wet, stands the ground
that one day will stand him.
What is there not to love?
Frogs and toads switch on, and—
there they are as if the first stars—
the fireflies revolving around him,
the universe's center still unspooling.

Reparations

I fix the fence the mare broke through,
restringing five lines of barbed wire
and trading out a post weakened from rot. She's cut;
flies swarm blood leaking from her sides,
her thighs, down her legs. She's left a trail
of herself over grass and sand, and,
uncomfortable with sting, paws
the ground and hovers near: how is it
I don't fear this thing of many claws?

We're lucky the wire had not caught
and tangled, tripping her and, rolling
as horses panicked do, wrapping as wire will.
Lucky it all came apart, that she had not
made herself a knot only a bullet could untie.
I've watched ranchers with cattle, a jacket cowling
an animal's head, picking barbs clean
as one might sandburs out of socks.
Tame as cattle may be, they thrash, too.

Imagine, then, the horse, wild still wild inside them,
prey's instinct commanding flight:
there are lions in those brambles, wolves' teeth.
Where she'd let me touch, I've applied a balm,
but the breeze, blowing across the east pond,
is luckier and cool. Summer heat, a galvanized coil
you're wound in, debilitates the calm
a man and horse need of each other.
As I make reparation, no gloves or sleeves for me:

a scar is a brand I can wear to be like horse.
The hammer works staples into new wood

odorous with creosote, and pliers lever wires
until they sing a harmony of hooves and hands
composed of ache, barbs like notes on a wire staff,
a range where we might go should we break through.

Dog Bite

The leg is white ground
where a hole has been punched
as by a stick carved sharp
with a pocket knife.
How pretty the bloom
that leaps from the quick seed:
the bruise's blush, the blood
sprouting like fragrance.

Cold Front, September

Listen: The wind draws the leaves
from the lawn upward and back into the oak limbs
they fell from. A clatter there,
as if someone rattling a door to a house
where a neighbor slept away deeply the day's doldrums.
Suddenly the astonished mass rushes to rise to answer.

Across the hollow a hound complains,
and others respond until the woods
sing the cold, crisp news. The horses in the pasture,
feeling the thrill of it, toss their heads,
rear and run hard on harder ground.
There's rain building far West, clouds there
black and wrapped in strings of light,
but thunder rumbling here already.

Frost at First Sun

The pasture glazed silver,
the horses hold the night's black.
Steam lifts, and hands of ghosts
wash them true and into color.

Jed, Last February

The horse will not walk or stand but drops
to his knees, his great bulk going down
slowly, a heavy window swelled in its old frame.
I do what I can to keep the air, cold as it is, moving,
but the house he is, room by room, shuts itself up,
then tumbles like old walls pressed by a roof
as heavy as sky.
                              Damp grass where he lies
slips upward through winter mud, so many little promises
crushed. Clouds course his eyes, and—what is there to do
            but listen?
Breath, in and out. Breath, slower and
more slowly, and, like an old horse myself,
I kneel on the ground, awaiting the one intractable faith.

Fog on Farm Road Woods

They come—the woods marching
from thick white, first their leafy heads
and then their arms and the armored rest.
Every rank and file forward: sweet gum
and saw-tooth oak, yaupon and mimosa.
Those behind still cloaked, invisible still.

Cardinals like arrows tipped in fire;
warblers whirring matins to shield against
what might impend.
                                        When Birnam's
oaks and lindens trembled toward him,
Macbeth understood limbs
and tangles, all those thorny brambles.
Destiny's out there, coming on in sun.

Beatitudes, June Dusk

Blessed is the horse, head bowed, in deep Bermuda,
pond frogs decreeing day's end, egrets lifting
and falling like snow despite the warm breeze.

Blessed are his ears, shifting forward, back,
checking the approach of nothing,
blessed the tail brushing off nuisance,
and his eyes, soft as dusk, closing.

Night Walk on Farm Road

The night washes itself of dust
and comes out sparkling,
and farm lights, like stars,
guide us home. Damp, cold gravel
shuffles beneath our feet,
and locusts, those little tractors,
work the dark fields around us.

Burying the Dog

I bury the dog and plant a pecan tree
upon him, then rise to wash off what I have
left of him, the red clay that slakes
my arms and clothes, the flush that feels like heat,
and let the water fall upon the plot,
to start the tree, to hurry the dog
on his way to earth. I tell my wife,
who stands nearby, eyes deep wells of blue
I could drown in, the irony:
we feed the squirrels that drove him nuts
nuts that grow from him.
He'll chase them now from their insides.
She doesn't laugh at all.

Three heron, flying east to the neighbor's pond,
sloop low overhead and one, curious perhaps,
circles back and squawks, indignant.
He tips his wings and wings away. What was he looking for?
We watch the living fossil sail, but he's not going
to the place the others are, flying as if he's lost.
I suspect there's a joke here, too,
but I catch a momentary balance
steeped in silence as the ground rolls under me.

Across Farm Road

At the neighbor's pond, kids near pickups
whoop and holler, skipping stones across the calm.
My horses watch and wait and worry,
ears lobbed forward, instinct a pulse
in their legs, shoulders, flanks, a bolt to open meadows
or steep inclines a predator could not comfortably crawl,
shale on slopes, cascades of stone to bring a charge quiet.
Here, inside perimeters of post and wire,
the flat blue-green of pasture, no haven
save shady trees or lean-tos to shield them.
My horses stare, and I join them,
watching what they worry over.
Noise skips and sinks into the tubs of our ears.
We stand our furious ground.

Garden Report

I move stones from stacks upon pallets,
two bulky loaves at a time, and bear them
to their places on the flowerbed borders.
Bottle brush, lantana, four o'clocks,
elephant ears, hostas—so many names
to memorize it's a chore. *It's a labor of love,*
my wife insists, as she has each weekend
this past year, *to put your back into the beauty*
of the garden. She's plotting hummingbirds in bushes,
cardinals and buntings, swallowtails and monarchs.
We're giving back what we've been given.
First-father Adam, by sweat of his brow,
moved boulders bigger than Eternity
to please his miscreant wife.
I have a half acre nearly done, three times
that much to go: peach trees and pears,
blueberries and figs. *No apple trees,*
she directs. *It's too hot for them here.*
A ton of stones ridden atop my belly
to contain the perennials—blue plumbago
and firebush, verbena, pavonia, and bouncing bet;
my hands molded into red bricks.
I hope for deep blooms outnumbering
the holes I've dug to root them, birds
as many as the gravel one rock might make
hammered down, butterflies flitting
among petals, wings like fingers, overworked,
flexing. Then, sitting still.

Thunderstorm on Farm Road

I stand at the center of the road the weather paves,
rain like a roller laying flat the county's blacktop,
to once again lead the horses to stall and calm, to abate them
with hay and oats, the sweet and sleepy dust.
Scrub oak and sweet gum, jack pine and locust,
knocked about, bullied, twist and struggle
in the grip and eddy of the air's deepening river.
Limbs crack, as they always do in these storms.
Upturned roots rip the weave of red dirt
and coastal grass. Best to bend in drench and chill
as you can, like blind Samson feeling his way,
lifting to the storm's lift, and, like thunder
and pang of light, groaning from habit.

Owls, Near Midnight

Three owls decree boundaries,
the first down a draw, inside black thicket,
a second east past the neighbor's pond
where egrets rest among moaning cattle.
The third sits a snag above our garden
as rabbits mole among the plants
and toads serenade the perfection of moonlessness.

Beside me, the new puppy yawns, nervous;
cocks his head at each sounding, unsure
if he should run or bark (though
there are other things I wish he'd do).
The night clear, a thousand owls
blink down at us, wait and prowl
where lines of trespass end
and claims dissipate, as night always does,
with first and foremost light.

Sleeping with Dogs

The king-sized bed is a raft adrift black water
where two people and their little dogs, snoring,
huddle and shiver beneath the ceiling fan's whir;
the room, smeared with shadows, a bower of limbs
and quaking leaves overhead. What riverboat sank
to launch this consortium of legs, of mouths
puffing against drowning? What rough weather
or undercurrent snag spilled this cargo?

Some nights the river steers them through storms,
strobes setting woods ablaze, thunder growling.
Or moonlight blanches window sheers,
owls and coyotes coughing like old men restless, haunted
not of departures—there have been so many—
but of destinations. Shacks and cobbled piers
near reedy banks, flutes whistling;
lonely, beautiful cities gambling light and music and hurt.

The delta widens, seeps into a gulf. Here we go:
penniless as leaves cupped like hands,
steamer trunks full of cares bobbing in the wake.
The sleeping dogs, their ears alert, poised to leap,
to swim the river's push, let it dare, to protect.
Unaware of smallness, so big their dreams.
And old lovers, desolate of need, willing to drown together.

Armadillo on the Tall Lawn, 4 A.M.

The armadillo, under moonlight, lumbers like a tank
through dew-tipped grass, slapping crickets
and fireflies down. Grandma warned me,
as a child, that crickets were lucky: *Leave them alone*
or you'll wish you had. What I wish, at my age now,
is that I was lucky enough to still hear their chirpings.
The annoyance had once provoked my deafness to prophecy.

And the armadillo's pursuit of fireflies as that boy's was,
summering and tempting fate on that grandmother's farm,
pulling them from consuming dark, inches before his face,
above his head. Their appearances and disappearances
little lighthouse beacons on a foggy shore,
rocks concealed under waves, the light so faint,
the shipwreck imminent unless the light was caught and freed.
Inside cupped fists, their fuses lit the explosion
that lit the universe and everything was safe, everything quiet.

Tonight, the dog beside me at the fence barks and barks:
the armadillo has come to nub out grubs and worms,
but gotten luckier. So sure and undisturbed, despite our noise;
dancing in the rye just past our reach, he claws up ground,
            paws down air.
There tumble tiny lamps. There bits of fortune douse.

The Slope

for Nathan and Adelle

Down the back slope rain is white shadow
on pin oak and jack pine which rock with wind
so small you think of those years ago,
walking feet to numbness on cold floors,
winter and limbs gnawing the roof,
until the baby in your arms sleeps.
The rain is like that sleep coming on, far enough out there
you doubt its coming, it may just be fog.
Close enough you feel its sifting down, eyes closing.
An infant's sigh, and there rain is, thick as slumber.

The Cannas

Blooms like battle plumes over her head,
the pug pokes out her flat face from between big leaves,
waits to ambush her sister stomping heavily by.
The hidden one crouches, black inside the shadows
of sun-reaching flowers.
                                        A poet friend once warned:
you can't write poems about dogs—it's the death of poetry,
ask Browning or Arnold. But it's not about dogs so much
as cannas, red and orange, green-leafed and chocolate,
towers of a castle on fire,
                                        and less about cannas
than pathways coursed, as a boy, inside my father's corner patch,
my own sister, her heart diseased, months from death,
plodding toward the swing where she flew until she'd vomit.
My assault awaited her, summer cooler under the cannas'
        dark umbrella.
Leaping out at her, we'd scream delight, race a circle around
        the house
that left her breathless.
                                        She'd sit and I'd run for the both of us.
As perhaps I still do, these years later. Like a dog's tenacity,
locking jaws onto a rope or sock and pulling for all its worth.
The cannas swing on small winds, blooms like tongues
as much as flames, leaves hands and arms waving goodbye or hello,
anyway you look at it, perennial.

Late Evening, November Sleet

Suffice it to say

if the world stopped now—the oak
ablaze in the pit while sleet sizzles
and disappears as it hits the embers;
and the breeze, near freeze, seeps
inside the folds of my jacket—
I am so close to sleep the going
would not be so horrible here
among elements I understand.
And the ground I am coming to—the one sure thing,
as it always is about ash, drench or ice, the air's rimple—
like an old man with his pipe,
drawing in smoke, puffing out rings of life.

Beatitudes, Again: The Horse Lesson, July Nightfall

for Don Welch

Blessed is the man, his head bowed now
in the manner of his horses, standing in blue grass
among the quiet giants, listening to pond frogs,
cicadas, the distant thunder that hums in heat.

Blessed the heaviness they have no choice but carry,
the warm wind washing well away
the nuisance of thought; blessed the nothing that settles
upon their ears, the dust that settles all questions,

the oncoming dark, pierced by so many stars,
like doubt turned to grace.

ACKNOWLEDGMENTS

I am grateful to the editors of the following magazines where some of these poems, or earlier versions of them, appeared:

Antigonish Review: "Planning the Affair," "The Poem."
Big Muddy: "My Son, at Post, Camp Victory, Baghdad," "The Poets."
Blue Unicorn: "Finding the Homestead House, 1963," "Night Walk on Farm Road."
Borderlands: "My Children's Inheritance."
The Briar Cliff Review: "Photograph of Three Sisters, 1954," "Split, 1992."
Chariton Review: "American History," "The Ball Game, 1975," "The Cowley County Murders, 1959 (The Deputy's Report)," "The Last Night," "No Accounts, 1948," "The World."
Contemporary Verse 2: "The Evening News."
Dalhousie Review: "Little Sahara," "The Rock Hound," "The Yawn."
The Fiddlehead: "The Death of the Vaudevillian," "December 1944," "Passing the Bottle," "Sitting on Foth's Roof, with Beer," "Villanelle for Nathan," "The Suicide."
Fugue: "Traveling to the Big Empty."
Great River Review: "Butchering Chickens."
Jabberwock Review: "Why We Bought a Horse," "Meteor Shower, with Horses."
Kansas Quarterly: "February Wash," "Anniversary," "Assets, 1987."
Louisiana Literature: "The Slope," "The Big Empty."
The Midwest Quarterly: "Children of the Clouds," "The Cranes, Texas January," "For My Sister, 1961," "Pancakes," "Plain Sense," "These Children," "108°—The Horse Pasture," "Anecdote of the Horses," "Beatitudes, June Dusk," "Feeding Horses, During Snow," "Frost at First Sun," "Grace, This Spring," "The High Desert, Idaho, September," "Horses, Considering Winter," "Idaho Farm, June 2004," "Nine Choruses, in Which Horses Play a Part," "Physics," "Thunderstorm on Farm Road," "Cold Front, September," "Reparations."
Montserrat Review: "On Seeing the Ex-Wife," "Prayer After Sex."
New Mexico Humanities Review: "Night Fishing on Missouri's James River," "Bladen, Nebraska."

North Dakota Quarterly: "The Move to Tarkio, Missouri, 1985."
Passages North: "Anna Cernik's Diary: Of Daughters and Sons."
Phantasmagoria: "The Fiction of Place."
Pinch: "Anxiety."
Pinyon: "The Heart."
Plainsong: "American Flyer."
Poetry East: "On Horseback, Hell's Gate Canyon, October," "Vigil at a Missile Silo."
Poetry Nottingham: "Last Practice."
Poetry Wales: "The Company Representative and the Trainee," "The Oasis Bar."
Portland Review: "Syllogism: On Highway 12, Clearwater River."
Prairie Schooner: "The Creighton Pool Hall," "Custody," "Digging for Fossils."
River City: "For Travis, Disappointed by First Love," "Hands," "Windows."
River Styx: "The Horse Considers Hell."
Shenandoah: "In Hurricane, with Horses," "Early Morning on Farm Road," "A Thousand Reasons."
Solo: "Surviving."
South Dakota Review: "Elms."
Water-Stone Review: "Conditions of Grace."
Westview: "Before We Lost Our Ways."
The Windsor Review: "The Old School."

"No Accounts, 1948" was included in *Jumping Pond: Poems and Stories from the Ozarks* (Southwest Missouri State U, 1983).

"Anna Cernik's Diary: Of Daughters and Sons" was also included in the 1985 *Anthology of Magazine Verse & Yearbook of American Poetry*; and, in *Passages North Anthology: A Decade of Good Writing* (Milkweed Editions, 1990).

"The Death of the Vaudevillian" was included in *Sometime the Cow Kick Your Head: The Biennial of Light Verse & Witty Poems, '88/'89* (Bits Press, 1988).

"Self-Portrait" was first published in *As Far as I Can See: Contemporary Writing from the Middle Plains* (Windflower Press, 1989).

"The Rock Hound," "The Old School," and "Sitting on Foth's Roof, with Beer" were included in *Poetry of Nebraska* (a special issue of the *Nebraska English Journal*, 1989).

"Vigil at a Missile Silo" was reprinted in *Atomic Ghost: Poets Respond to the Nuclear Age* (Coffee House Press, 1995); and, in *The Fire Next Time: Faith and the Future of Nuclear Weapons* (a special issue of *Reflections: Yale Divinity School*, 2009).

"The Creighton Pool Hall," "The Poem," "Villanelle for Nathan," and "The World" were reprinted in *The Logan House Anthology of 21st Century American Poetry* (Logan House Press, 2001).

"Custody," "Talking November Weather, Long Distance," and "Death's Door" were included in *Nebraska Presence: An Anthology of Poetry* (Backwaters Press, 2007).

"On Horseback, Hell's Gate Canyon, October," "Why We Bought a Horse," and "Feeding Horses, During Snow" were published in *Cadence of Hooves: A Celebration of Horses* (Yarroway Mountain Press, 2008).

"How to Know There's Actually a Heaven" was included in *Three Generations of Nebraska Poets*, a special issue of *The Midwest Quarterly* (Summer 2011).

"The Brain-Eaters" was issued as a limited-edition, over-sized broadside by Denise Brady and the Kimmel Harding Nelson Center for the Arts, 2003.

Selected poems, some of them revised for *Conditions of Grace*, are taken from the following volumes:

The Suicide (Cummington Press, 1988); *Before We Lost Our Ways* (Hurākan/College of the Mainland, 1996); *Here in the Big Empty* (Backwaters Press, 2006); and, *Landscapes, with Horses* (LaNana Creek Press, 2012).

Thanks, in particular, to Greg Kosmicki of Backwaters Press and Charles Jones of LaNana Creek Press. Thanks also to these individuals who made suggestions on poems that appeared in *Before We Lost Our Ways* and *Here in the Big Empty,* specifically the late William Kloefkorn, Don Welch, Greg Kuzma, Kelly Cherry, Pat Sturm, Rich Wyatt, Marjorie Saiser, and Barbara Schmitz. Much appreciation to Claire Davis, Greg Kuzma, and Steve Davenport for their insights on new and previously uncollected pieces and to Larry D. Thomas, Don Welch, Stephen Meats, David Baker, and R. T. Smith for their endorsement of this book.

Especial thanks to my wife, Kimberly Verhines, whose critical eye and sound judgment guided me to the best of my work.